DEVELOPING AN INTEGRATED MARKETING PLAN

FIRST EDITION

D1622857

by **Eric Stewart Harvey**
Ball State University

Bassim Hamadeh, CEO and Publisher

Kassie Graves, Director of Acquisitions

Jamie Giganti, Senior Managing Editor

Miguel Macias, Senior Graphic Designer

Angela Schultz, Senior Field Acquisitions Editor

Michelle Piehl, Project Editor

Alexa Lucido, Licensing Coordinator

Rachel Singer, Associate Editor

Kevin Fontimayor, Interior Designer

Copyright © 2017 by Cognella, Inc. All rights reserved. No part of this publication may be reprinted, reproduced, transmitted, or utilized in any form or by any electronic, mechanical, or other means, now known or hereafter invented, including photocopying, microfilming, and recording, or in any information retrieval system without the written permission of Cognella, Inc.

Trademark Notice: Product or corporate names may be trademarks or registered trademarks, and are used only for identification and explanation without intent to infringe.

Cover image copyright © 2016 iStockphoto LP/themacz

Printed in the United States of America

ISBN: 978-1-63487-925-5 (pbk) / 978-1-63487-926-2 (br)

This book will provide you with a strategic process for creating an integrated marketing communications plan, and give you a good understanding of integrated marketing communications (IMC).

In addition to providing a thorough understanding of integrated marketing communications (IMC), this book will also provide you with a strategic process for creating an integrated marketing communication plan.

TABLE of CONTENTS

1

What is IMC?

MAIN IDEAS

- What is IMC and how does it play in today's marketing communication environment?

- The evolution of media and how traditional digital media shares the marketplace.

- What can media platforms do for your campaign?

- Outlining a traditional integrated marketing communication plan.

An Integrated Marketing Communications (IMC) approach entails having many different marketing techniques that are combined and coordinated across various channels in order to deliver transparent, reliable messages about the company, product, or service.

Marketing attempts have moved away from high-cost mass advertising to more focused cross-channel marketing. Marketers are using IMC to create campaigns that are cost-effective and can deliver value to the consumer. IMC can save many marketers valuable time by narrowing the focus to the best possible marketing tool.

Integrated Marketing Communications is a methodology organizations use to harmonize marketing attempts across numerous communication mediums. The goal of IMC is to organize marketing elements such as advertising, sales promotion, customer service, public relations, direct marketing, and sales support.

ADVERTISING

Advertising is considered one of the most effective methods of brand promotion. Advertising helps companies attract a broader audience in a short period of time. Depending on what particular advertisements are selected for radio, television, newspaper or Out of Home (OOH), the goal is to convince customers to buy and worship the brand. Advertisements take the customer through the process of awareness, comprehension, conviction, desire, and action.

SALES PROMOTION

Sales promotion is creating ways to have a direct affect on brands (products and services). Promotion is a way to work through channels by using a strategy like discounting methods where couponing is often used. Retention strategy's are often using loyalty programs and memberships providing incentives that will entice customers with the right approach to maintain that brand loyalty.

DIRECT MARKETING

Direct marketing provides companies with a way to connect directly with customers. Today, direct marketing can be elevated through the use of marketing automation software, email, letters brochures, catalogues, and text messages.

PERSONAL SELLING

Personal selling is considered one of the most effective IMC tools for reaching customers. This strategy requires proper training of a skilled sales person who masters the product or service. The biggest reward in this process is developing, strengthening, or maintaining customer relationships.

PUBLIC RELATION ACTIVITIES

Public relation activities can be a good way to streamline your budget and get the word out through the news, events, press releases, or even public appearances.

Traditional and Digital Marketing

IMC tools apply to both traditional (offline) and digital (online) marketing environments. Traditional marketing may require significant resources to get preferred outcomes. Examples of traditional media include television, radio, newspapers, magazines, posters, brochures, and billboards. Digital marketing, on the other hand, provides functionalities that traditional marketing does not efficiently cover. Digital marketing, as defined by The Gartner Group, continues to be integrated with multichannel campaign management, includes addressable branding/advertising, contextual marketing, social marketing, and transactional marketing. Digital marketing extends the marketing process through channels such as the Web, video, mobile and social applications, point-of-sale terminals, digital signage, and kiosks.

I have created an outline to help with staying on task.

Integrated marketing campaigns can be a complicated science to perfect.

The marketing dynamics in today's world presents no structured environment. Most marketers are looking for that new shiny object. Having a plan in todays environment is essential for marketers to direct there marketing activities.

The IMC plan outline will give marketers a since of stability through the process. You will see in the book that each area is dependent with other areas in the outline. It will be a critical step that you follow the process to have a very successful campaign.

Figure 1.0. Traditional and Digital Marketing

TRADITIONAL	DIGITAL
Print	Desktop Website
TV	Mobile Website
Radio	Mobile Apps
Newspaper	Social Media
OOH–Billboards	Digital signage
Magazines	Video
Brochures	Interactives

EXECUTIVE SUMMARY

An executive summary will provide a short summary of the situation analysis along with recommendations included in the IMC plan. The size of the executive summary is about one page or less in length.

SITUATION ANALYSIS

This component of the IMC plan will assess the overall environment, market, and industry facing the company or organization. In this section, you will be looking for hard data, facts, and assumptions regarding the company, product, customers, competitors and environmental factors. This area will set the stage for the plan and give you a great foundation for a planning process.

Figure 1.1. IMC Outline

IMC Outline

1. Executive Summary
2. Situation Analysis
   a. Environmental Analysis
   b. Company Analysis
   c. Product Analysis
   d. Consumer Analysis
   e. Competitive Analysis
3. SWOT Analysis
4. Analysis of Research
5. Target Market Profile
6. Objectives
   a. Marketing objectives
   b. IMC objectives
   c. Media objectives
7. Program Strategies
   a. Marketing strategies
   b. IMC strategies
   c. Media strategies
8. Media Plan
   a. Media Schedule
   b. Media Mix
9. Budget
10. Evaluation
   a. Pre- and Post-Testing Efforts
11. Appendices
   a. Research
   b. Creative

SWOT ANALYSIS

The SWOT analysis is the backbone of the situation analysis and will help organize information about the company, product, customer, competitor and environmental factors. SWOT is the abbreviation of Strengths, Weaknesses, Opportunities, and Threats.

RESEARCH ANALYSIS

In this section you will discuss how the data was collected and focus on the findings. This analysis will help you establish credibility.

TARGET MARKET PROFILE

In this section, you will identify a concise description of your consumer prospect by using demographic and psychographic information.

OBJECTIVES

In this section, provide measurable and achievable marketing, IMC, and media objectives on what you want to achieve.

PROGRAM STRATEGIES

In this section, provide marketing, IMC, and media strategies to achieve those objectives. Discuss your "big idea" and major messaging. How are you planning to reach and persuade a customer to buy a product or a service?

MEDIA PLAN

Select the media that is cost effective for advertising to your target audience. Describe the strategy, tactics, and necessary allocation of resources. Then, describe the media schedule and mix that will address your target audience.

BUDGET

Include the detailed cost of your IMC plan, along with adequate timing of these expenses. This part of the plan may also include charts and graphs to show costs by month or quarters.

EVALUATION AND CONTROL

Discuss how you will evaluate the IMC plan or campaign and what provisions are in place to make adjustments.

APPENDICES

This section should include all or most of the information you have generated, from research to creative. The client may wish to see any information that would be relevant to the plan.

References

1. Krishan Kant, "Integrated Marketing Communications (IMC)," *Articlesbase,* last modified January 13, 2011, http://www. articlesbase.com/marketing-tips-articles/integrated-marketing-management-imc-4029166.html.

2. "Integrated Marketing Communications Tools," *Management Study Guide,* accessed April 3, 2015, http://management-studyguide.com/integrated-marketing-communication-tools.htm.

3. First name, Last name. *Ayer's Dictionary of Advertising Terms* (Philadelphia: Ayer Press, 1976), page number.

4. "Situation Analysis", *American Marketing Association,* accessed April 3, 2015, https://www.ama.org/resources/Pages/ Dictionary.aspx.

5. "Digital Marketing," *Gartner,* accessed April 15, 2015, http://www.gartner.com/it-glossary/digital-marketing.

2

THE ANALYSIS OF YOUR RESEARCH

MAIN IDEAS

This chapter will provide you with the best solutions for primary and secondary research.

- Start with secondary research to determine what information you already have that is readily available and where to look.

- After determining your secondary findings, then establish what is necessary for your primary research.

- Focus groups, observations, interviewing and surveys.

THE ANALYSIS OF YOUR RESEARCH

I n IMC today it is so important that you get critical information about your campaign or plan. IMC research is considered to be a strategic part of the process that is necessary for many reasons. This research will help you gather your thoughts about creating the plan. You will be looking for information that will help uncover critical IMC decisions. Areas of research include evaluating current messaging strategy to create a "big idea," what existing campaigns or promotions marketers have used, or even looking at the success of current or previous strategies. All of this information will be essential to the creation of your IMC plan.

Without taking an extensive look into the whole marketing research process, I will just provide you with some basic essentials. The two basic types of research are primary research and secondary research.

The direct goal of **secondary research** is to analyze already published data. Secondary data gives you the opportunity to identify specific competitors, establish benchmarks, and identify target segments. The selected segments you choose are the people who fall into your targeted demographic: people who live a certain lifestyle, exhibit particular behavioral patterns, or fall into predetermined age groups. Sources for secondary research include existing market research results, public information from Internet search engines, company or customer relations databases, or libraries. This information can help establish your situation analysis for the IMC plan by creating strategies for benchmarking, and helps determine the market segments that a company should target. Secondary research gives you an opportunity to make the most out of existing information available in your market. Consider using secondary research to gather an initial understanding of your industry. However, you must be careful with secondary research, especially when compiling and interpreting the information. It is key that you clearly understand what business sector or industry they participating. If you are in the wrong market segment, the research will be irrelevant. Instead of relying only on secondary research, use the information you gather to establish a basis for your primary source research. Also, remember that secondary resources can be dated. Avoid using only online resources. Doing so can eliminate offline resources that could be relevant to your research objectives. Web resources are often outdated. Consider the library as an alternative source. After gathering all of your data it is important to assess the information to see what you are missing. Then you can better plan your primary research to fill in these gaps.

The goal of **primary research** is to create your own information. Primary research will allow you to instantaneously feel more in control of your project. Through this qualitative research process, you can collect research through interviews, surveys, questionnaires, focus groups, and field tests. The primary research approach provides a more thorough delivery of information. Although primary research gives you control over your project, it is more expensive and time consuming than using the secondary research method. Using only primary research creates a sometimes lengthy and time-consuming process. It may take a lot of time if you are inexperienced in refining or even producing surveys, questionnaires, or gaining access to a quality sample. Today, with social media, there are plenty of more efficient primary research opportunities to explore with Facebook, Twitter, and Instagram. Choosing the primary research method is best once you have exhausted secondary research methods. Focusing first on secondary research will make the gaps in your research much clearer.

Library resources for the IMC plan: Most university libraries have excellent sources to help you with researching needed information. You will see several resources that can assist you in searching for the required information.

Figure 2.0. Marketing Research: Primary and Secondary Research Examples

PRIMARY RESEARCH: EXAMPLES	SECONDARY RESEARCH: EXAMPLES
Focus Groups: Organizing a group of people from similar segments. Placing them in a setting that allows for asking perceptive questions about uncovered information from the secondary resources.	**Internal Sources:** Normally these resources are located in the client's information systems locations, such as data warehouses, databases, or archival filing systems.
Surveys: Surveys are another choice of primary research that can be effective and efficient. Surveys are a small or large sample of questions focused on getting feedback from a targeted segment. Most surveys can be distributed by paper or electronic means such as email. Qualtrics or SurveyMonkey are survey services with easy setup and capabilities to help with analysis.	**Samples:** Most financial documents can be considered the best sources ; Balance sheets, profit and loss statements, inventory records and sales figures.
Observation: Non-evasive research methods include watching individuals complete a process and recording observations. An alternative could be a staged situation with the subject(s) aware of the monitoring process.	**External sources:** In the event that internal sources do not have enough relevance, you should look outside of the client's business marketplace. Other businesses in the same industry could have similar information that may be relevant in this situation.

(continued)

PRIMARY RESEARCH: EXAMPLES	SECONDARY RESEARCH: EXAMPLES
Testing or Experimentation: This technique, which may or may not be controlled, is a scientific test. The experiment method will use hypotheses and variables to determine the outcome.	**Samples:** External sources consider the following sampled information: Competitor information, internet sources, universities or colleges and government sources.
In-depth Interviews: This method is similar to the focus group concept, but involves one moderator asking multiple questions to one person in a private interviewing session.	

After completing the marketing research for your IMC plan, it is critical to take notes on what was accomplished. The analysis of your research is an important component of your IMC plan. You will want to describe how, when, where, and by whom the data was collected.

Figure 2.1. Marketing Decisions and Types of Research

MARKETING DECISION	TYPES OF RESEARCH
Target Markets	sales, market size, demand for product, customer characteristics, purchase behavior, customer satisfaction, website traffic
Product	product development, package protection, packaging awareness, brand name selection, brand recognition, brand preference, product positioning
Distribution	distributor interest, assessing shipping options, online shopping, retail store site selection
Promotion	advertising recall, advertising copy testing, sales promotion response rates, sales force compensation, traffic studies (outdoor advertising), public relations media placement
Pricing	price elasticity analysis, optimal price setting, discount options
External Factors	competitive analysis, legal environment, social and cultural trends
Other	company image, test marketing

It is also important to break down your secondary research into three sections: secondary consumer research, trade research, and other research. Feel free to provide any marketing insights that stuck out during your research process. You should discuss findings that will help your campaign or were surprisingly unexpected.

The table on the next page presents a small sampling of the types of research that can influence specific marketing decisions.

Generally it is easier to do research on a company that is either publicly traded or a Fortune 500 company. Before you select your company, you might want to do a little research to see what information is available. Use the sources below to investigate the company.

LexisNexis Academic— Comprehensive, authoritative news content, including current coverage and deep archives.

Business Source Premier—Use the Company Profiles to find basic information about your company.

Environmental Analysis

Business Source Premier—Includes articles helpful for researching the environment of an industry, trends that affect the buying minds of the consumer, as well as social, economic, and political factors.
Standard and Poor's Net Advantage—Includes news reports about trends and events in the industry, as well as information about companies in the industry.

Company, Industry, and Market Analysis

Business Source Premier—Try searching your company's name, your product name, or use the phrase "product lines." You may have to be creative!
Your Company's Website—Search for your company on Google. The website may have an investor's information link or a link to their mission statement.

Product Analysis

Market Share Reporter—Provides a compilation of market share reports from periodical literature and is a unique resource for competitive analysis, diversification planning, marketing research, and other forms of economic and policy analysis.
Standard and Poor's Net Advantage—See the Trends section of the Industry Survey Reports, which may include market share information.
Business Source Premier—Search for articles about your brand. For articles related to the product's life cycle, use search terms such as "life cycle" and "product recovery."
Gale Virtual Reference Library—Try searching for the *International Directory of Company Histories,* which discusses brands and companies.

Consumer Analysis

Mintel Reports—Designed to provide you with market analyses to get ahead of the competition. See reports from a particular sector, or about a demographic such as millennials, kids, or mothers.
Prizm Nielson—Evaluates market segments by linking consumer behaviors for shopping, financial, media and much more, to gain powerful insights that allow you to create actionable strategies and tactically execute while benchmarking your performance.
SRDS (Standard Rate and Data Service)—Find advertising rates for newspapers, magazines, and the internet.
Business Source Premier—This database also contains articles about consumers. Combine your brand or company with words like "consumer," "customer," or "marketing." You might also search for using terms to describe types of consumers, such as "millennials."

Encyclopedia of Major Marketing Campaigns, Volume 2 Online—A companion to the publisher's *Major Marketing Campaigns Annual*, this volume profiles five hundred of the most notable marketing and advertising campaigns of the past one hundred years.

Competitive Analysis

Market Share Reporter—Once you have located the market share for your product you will see a list of other competing products.

Standard and Poor's Net Advantage—Check the Industry Trends section for surveys that may include market share and sales figures.

Business Source Premier—Articles about your product or type of product may be helpful. Do a search using your product name or type.

LexisNexis Academic—Search under "Get Company Info" to find the Company Dossier. This source will help you find a list of competitors and financial information for the SWOT Analysis.

SWOT Analysis

Mintel Reports—Reports may give insight into what consumers want in a brand and how they think.

Business Source Premier—This is a key business database that includes over one thousand scholarly, peer-reviewed journals, as well as many popular business magazines and newspapers.

EDGAR—Form 10-K reports may contain valuable information related to this section of your paper. Enter your company's ticker symbol in the "Fast Search" box and look for the most recent 10-K filing.

Target Market Profile

Mintel Reports—See the Demographics column of the Category Overview. You might also search using keywords to describe your demographic or terms related to it.

Business Source Premier—Search using terms to describe the target market ("millennials" for example). Combine those terms with psychographics, psychology, demographics, or demography. You might also try using terms such as "education," or "income."

Cardcat -Try searching terms such as "market research," "consumer behavior," or "target marketing." You might combine those terms with any of the following terms: "GenX," "GenY," "Traditionalist," "Silent Generation," "Baby Boomers," "Travellers," or "Urbanites."

This style guide can be referenced at http://bsu.libguides.com/MKG420.

The chapter has provided some very good resources to completing an analysis of your research.

References

1. "Market Research", *Queensland Government*, last modified October 2, 2014, https://www.business.qld.gov.au/business/starting/market-customer-research/market-research-basics/market-research-methods.

2. Leslie Spencer Pyle, "How to Do Market Research — The Basics," *Entrepreneur*, last modified September 23, 2010, http://www.entrepreneur.com/article/217345.

3. Anastasia, "Market Research Techniques: Primary and Secondary Market Research," *Cleverism*, last modified May 3, 2015, https://www.cleverism.com/market-research-techniques-primary-secondary.

4. "Examples of Research in Marketing," *KnowThis.com*, accessed May 23, 2015, http://www.knowthis.com/marketing-research/examples-of-research-in-marketing.

5. Jack Neff, "Jack Honomichl, Who Defined Market Research Industry, Dies at 85," *AdAge*, last modified December 10, 2013, http://adage.com/article/news/market-research-chronicler-jack-honomichl-dies-85/245626.

6. Business Source Premier, accessed April 3, 2016, http://bsu.libguides.com/c.php?g=378182&p=2568354

7. Lexis Nexis, accessed April 3, 2016, http://bsu.libguides.com/companyinfo

8. Mintel Report, accessed April 9, 2016, http://academic.mintel.com.proxy.bsu.edu/homepages/default/

9. "Market Share Reporter," *Gale*, accessed April 9, 2016, http://find.galegroup.com/gdl/help/GDLeDirMSRHelp.html.

10. "My Best Segments," *Nielsen*, accessed April 24, 2016, https://segmentationsolutions.nielsen.com/mybestsegments.

11. "SRDS Media Planning Platform," *Kantar Media*, accessed April 24, 2016, http://next.srds.com/home.

12. *Encyclopedia of Major Marketing Campaigns, Volume 2* Online accessed, March 28th 2015,http://bsu.libguides.com/MKG420

3

BEGIN THE PROCESS
OF THE SITUATION
ANALYSIS

MAIN IDEAS

Use the information on research tips from Chapter 2 to help in this exploration.

- **Company Analysis:** Provides a very brief depiction of your company or client's current and previous status.

- **Industry and Market Analysis:** Explore what particular industry you are in, including the industry market size and market share.

- **Environmental Analysis:** Provides a brief depiction of each environmental factor that will affect your industry or business: social, cultural, economic, or political.

This chapter sketches how the environment impacts the establishment. The plan is to begin the situational analysis by exploring the following topics: company, consumers, competitors, and environmental factors. You will need to pursue factual data that will help the reader clearly understand important elements that help set the basis for IMC development.

A situational analysis includes a thorough review of internal and external factors affecting a company, product, or service. It helps create an overview of the organization that will lead to a better interpretation of the factors that will impact its future.

After getting a good understanding of your marketing research strategy, you will begin to gather information about the situation analysis. In this chapter, we will review the company, market, and environmental portions of the situation analysis.

The situation analysis is a way to look at how things were in the past, how they currently exist today, and where they want to go in the future. It is important to understand what is going on both internally and externally. The first part of the situation analysis will look into the company. Provide a brief description of the company, client, or product/service. Look at their philosophy, mission statements, overall orientation, and how this product or service is positioned in the company. How is the product playing a part in the overall brand, revenue, or loss of company? The current situation of the company should be heavily investigated with no stones unturned.

Look prospectively at what this company has done in the past, what they are currently doing, and what direction they are moving in the future. Once you have finished reviewing the internal factors of the company, you begin to look at the external factors of the industry. Clearly you must understand the place of the company, product, and service in the marketplace. Begin to explore what is going on in the industry or marketplace. Find out who is leading in market size and share of competition. Indicate if there is a pattern of distribution, or if sales are cyclical, seasonal, national, or regional. What or if there is an opportunity for extended development? Again, you are setting the stage by gathering this information to help you determine your strategy.

The IMC plan requires reviewing environmental factors such as social, cultural, political, and economic trends that may affect consumer behavior.

When looking at social and cultural environmental factors, you must explore what affects consumer purchasing patterns. Social factors tend to reflect how individuals interact with daily lifestyles. Consider what is currently impacting today's social climate and how those factors impact your product or service. For example, suppose a news network broke a story about processed meat. Would that story change how society regards certain fast food restaurants? The news story certainly could impact buyer behavior. Cultural factors, on the other hand, include education, language,, religious beliefs, clothing, food choices, and how you perceive marriage and family roles.

The political environment provides an outlook on the overall political situation in the country. Not only will you look at the effect of domestic politics, but also how global politics inform our nation's decisions. In an evaluation of the political environment, you should consider how government legislation will and can impact your business. Staying current on upcoming bills, new laws, or tariffs will provide important insight on possible impacts. For example, net neutrality bills state that the government must treat all data on the Internet as the same. These bills will certainly impact many different industries, especially in the online streaming marketplace.

The analysis of economic environment will examine many developments that impact consumer confidence and the ability to purchase goods and services. This environmental scan of the economy will consider factors such as unemployment and interest rates. These two economic indicators are critical to consumer decisions such as whether they can afford to buy a house, clothes, or groceries. Will consumers want to save their money, invest, or spend on a luxury item? For example, if interest rates go up, would consumers stop going out to dinner, buying clothes, or going on vacation?

All of these environmental factors need to be addressed and documented so that you will have a clear approach to completing your IMC plan. These factors can impact your campaign significantly. Environmental factors are not in your control, so being aware of possible impacts is invaluable.

References

1. Kristie Lorette, "A Situational Analysis of a Strategic Marketing Plan," *Chron,* accessed May 30, 2015, http://smallbusiness.chron.com/situational-analysis-strategic-marketing-plan-1474.html.

2. Jim Makos, "What is Environmental Analysis," *Pestle Analysis,* modified February 23, 2015, http://pestleanalysis.com/what-is-environmental-analysis.

4

SITUATION ANALYSIS CONTINUED

MAIN IDEAS

- **Consumer Analysis:** Discuss the existing target market of the brand. Explore demographic and psychographical information. Establish what criteria people will use to make purchasing decisions. Are there any geographical differences among consumers?

- **Product Analysis:** Provide a very brief history of the brand. Discuss product features, benefits, physical attributes, brand personality, and the overall product life cycle.

This chapter continues the situation analysis by discussing the consumer and product analysis.

The consumer analysis section of the integrated marketing plan provides a detailed analysis of the customer market. Normally, only a few market segments are already established. However, in certain instances there are different market segments to consider. Understanding the consumer behavior of customers will help to segment the market. Having this information can help you determine target markets and develop a marketing mix that meets the demands or needs of customers.

Consumers are connecting and interacting with media and brands in more complex and appealing ways. Explore the lifestyles and demographics of your customers or consumers. Find out where they eat, sleep, and go to church. This useful information can lead to establishing personas or profiles and predicting consumer behavior. As mentioned previously, psychographic and demographical information is instrumental for a consumer analysis.

Let's look at a systematic way to approach consumer analysis.

Examining their general characteristics is an excellent way to describe consumers. Key categories of examination include:

1. **Demographic**: The most commonly used demographics are age, sex, geographic location, and stage in the life cycle. These characteristics are relatively easy to ascertain. Unfortunately, in many cases, demographic groups are not clearly differentiated in their behavior toward a product or service.

2. **Socioeconomic**: Socioeconomic variables include income and related variables such as education, occupation, and social class. Income and education are generally more useful variables to consider. As with demographics, the relationship between socioeconomic variables and purchase behavior can be weak.

3. **Personality**: Given the relatively limited predictive power of demographic and socioeconomic variables, the fact that many marketers are trained in psychology, and the natural desire to find a basis for profiling consumers that is useful across many situations, it is not surprising that marketers have attempted

Figure 4.0. Eight questions to help research your consumers

EIGHT QUESTIONS TO HELP RESEARCH YOUR CONSUMERS.
1. Who are the customers for this product or service?
2. What are customers buying and how do they use it?
3. Where do your customers go to buy products?
4. When are purchasing decisions made?
5. How do customers make purchasing decisions?
6. Why do customers choose a particular product?
7. How do customers respond to marketing programs such as advertising and promotions?
8. Will the consumer buy the product again?

to use personality traits as a basis for segmentation. Unfortunately, general personality variables have proven even less useful than demographic or socioeconomic variables in predicting purchasing behavior.

4. **Psychographics and values**: Psychographics represent an evolution from general personality variables to attitudes and behaviors more closely related to consumption of goods and services. Also know as lifestyle variables, psychographics generally fall into three categories: activities (e.g. fishing, knitting, golfing), interests (e.g. music, art), and opinions.

The **product analysis** gives a background of where the brand has been and where it wants to go in the future. The objective of a product analysis is to understand factors for success and failure, and to establish a foundation for an overall IMC strategy.

The first charge in analyzing the product is to become acquainted with the product.

- What does the product actually do?
- How does the product perform?
- What does the product look like?

Consider these questions and many more before completing the product analysis. When performing the product analysis, consider breaking your description of the product offerings into small categories:

- **Product Attributes** will describe the product marketing mix of branding strategies that identify product features and major benefits for individuals using the product.
- **Pricing** will describe the price marketing mix of strategies that address all levels of pricing, including discounts and incentives that are offered either to vendors, distributors, or end users.
- **Place** will describe the distribution aspect of the marketing mix that provides accessibility to the final user. The discussion of place should include which channels are used, benefits received by distributors, and how products are being shipped. Normally, the supply chain process is addressed in this section.
- **Promotion** will describe the promotional marketing mix strategy that addresses advertising, sales promotion, personal selling, public relations, and determines how the product

is currently positioned in the market. In this section you will also include the pre- and post-support services provided to product users.

The consumer and product analyses establish important background foundation for your situation analysis and will give you a brief snapshot of what your IMC plan may need.

References

1. Jana Lay-Hwa Bowden, "The Process of Customer Engagement: A Conceptual Framework," *Journal of Marketing Theory and Practice* 17 no. 1 (Winter 2009): 63–74.

2. "Study: Companies fail to understand their customers," *Advertising Age,* August 7, 2013, http://adage.com/article/btob/study-companies-fail-understand-customers/289958.

3. "My Best Segments," *PRIZM*, accessed June 2, 2015, http://www.nielsen.com/us/en.html

4. Donald R. Lehman and Russell S. Winer, *Product Management* (4 ed.) (New York: McGraw Hill/Irwin, 2005).

5

FINALIZING THE SITUATION ANALYSIS

MAIN IDEAS

- **Competitive Analysis:** Who are the competitors and what are there major attributes?

- **SWOT Analysis:** Evaluate the brand equity of your product. Is it strong or weak? In what areas? Define and describe the strengths, weaknesses, opportunities, and threats that your brand faces, and then discuss how you can utilize them for your marketing efforts.

T his chapter will focus on the **Competitive Analysis** and the **SWOT Analysis.**

The **competitive analysis** is one of the most significant components of any marketing plan. This evaluation establishes what will make your product and services distinctive. The information will help determine what qualities are important to entice your target market.

See below for a list of several elements to consider in your competitive analysis.

Figure 5.0. Competitive Analysis Evaluation Process

* Understand your industry scope, size, and character
* Who are your competitors? Are they leaders or followers?
* Who are the customers and what are their expectations?
* What are the critical success factors in this industry?

The fundamental objective of a competitive analysis is to gain enough information about competitors to help formulate the company's competitive strategy. This will give you insight into how your IMC plan will respond to the likely actions and responses of competitors.

A competitive analysis is a critical part of your IMC plan. After selecting your competitors, evaluate them by placing them into strategic groups showing how they compete in categories such as market share, product or services, profitability, marketing objectives, current and past strategies, and strengths and weaknesses.

Here are ten guiding questions to help you secure this key information:

1. Who are your competitors?
2. What is their financial status?
3. What products or services do they sell?
4. What is each competitor's market share?
5. What are their past marketing mix strategies?
6. What are their current marketing mix strategies?
7. What type of marketing communications are used to market their products or services?
8. What are the competitor's strengths and weaknesses?
9. What potential threats do your competitors pose?
10. What potential opportunities do they make available to you?

Putting this information into a matrix will provide a good visual for your client and also makes the data easier to analyze. A quick and easy way to compare your product or service with similar ones on the market is to make a competition grid.

Figure 5.1. Competitive Matrix

	INITIAL COMPANY	COMPETITOR #1	COMPETITOR #2	COMPETITOR #3
Who are your competitors?				
What is their financial status?				
What products or services do they sell?				
What is the market share?				
What are their past marketing mix strategies?				
What are their current marketing mix strategies?				
What type of marketing communications are used to market their products or services?				
What are the competitor's strengths and weaknesses?				
What potential threats do your competitors pose?				
What potential opportunities do they make available to you?				

Figure 5.2. Situation Analysis/SWOT

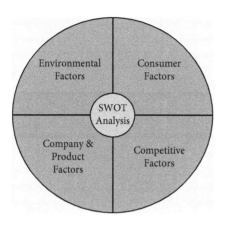

SWOT ANALYSIS

The **SWOT analysis** will evaluate the overall brand equity of your product or service. You will determine whether the product or service is strong or weak in the marketplace, what opportunities are present, and what threats may impact your status.

The SWOT analysis includes four key elements:

- **Strengths:** Qualities that display what the company does best and what makes your product or service successful.
- **Weaknesses:** Qualities that make your company unsuccessful. Weaknesses need special attention so that they do not spread to other areas of the business.
- **Opportunities:** External dynamics that can improve your position in the marketplace.
- **Threats:** External dynamics that can weaken your position in the marketplace.

See below for questions to guide your SWOT analysis.

Figure 5.3. SWOT Analysis

	GOOD–Useful	BAD–Damaging
Inside In-house	**S** Strengths	**W** Weaknesses
Outside External	**O** Opportunities	**T** Threats

Strengths

- What are your organization's core competencies?
- What do you do better than any other competitor?
- What strengths do others identify in your industry?
- What is your unique, cost-effective resource that others do not possess?

Weaknesses

- What is your biggest gap that needs improvement?
- What are you currently avoiding?
- What weaknesses do others identify in your industry?
- What aspects of your business are not profitable?

Opportunities

- What good prospects are obtainable?
- What stimulating developments are in the marketplace?
- What positive environmental factors are occurring?
- What are new customer needs?

Threats

- What are your biggest hurdles?
- What is happening in the competitive landscape?
- What are your current vulnerabilities?
- What negative environmental factors are occurring?
- Organizing your SWOT analysis information into a matrix provides an excellent way to visually analyze your competitors.

Figure 5.4. Competitive SWOT Matrix

	COMPANY	COMPETITOR #1	COMPETITOR #2	COMPETITOR #3
Strengths				
What are your organization's core competencies?				
What do you do better than any other competitor?				
What strengths do others identify in your industry?				
What is your unique, cost-effective resource that others do not possess?				
Weaknesses				
What is your biggest gap that needs improvement?				
What are you currently avoiding?				
What weaknesses do others identify in your industry?				
What aspects of your business are not profitable?				

(continued)

	COMPANY	COMPETITOR #1	COMPETITOR #2	COMPETITOR #3
Opportunities				
What good prospects are obtainable?				
What stimulating developments are in the marketplace?				
What positive environmental factors are occurring?				
What are new customer needs?				
Threats				
What are your biggest hurdles?				
What is happening in the competitive landscape?				
What are your current vulnerabilities?				
What negative environmental factors are occurring?				

Consider using these sources in Figure 5.5 to gather the necessary data for your SWOT analysis. These sources can help you establish a good foundation towards completing the SWOT.

Figure 5.5. SWOT Analysis—Where to Look for the Information

Background

- Get a good understanding of the company you are researching. Find out where the offices are located and examine their online presence. Learn about the history of the company by reviewing key dates, personalities, events, and trends. How is the company structured? Who owns the company?

(continued)

Financials

- Get a good understanding of the company's finances. Are they making money or losing money? Annual reports and 10-Ks are good sources for net income, balance sheets, and cash flow statements.

Products

- What are the key products that the company offers? Dig into the breadth and depth of the product lines. What markets are they performing in? Consider a BCG model to see where the product is positioned within the company. What patents or licenses are available?

Marketing

- What customer segments are served in their industry? Look at market share and consumer behavioral information. Based on demographic and or psychographic information, will customers in this market grow or decline?
- How much is spent on advertising and promotional budgets? Does the company have a specific advertising theme? Look at previous advertising success.
- Look at what channels are used to establish direct or indirect relationships. Are they intensive, exclusive, or specialized alliances? Any relation to geographical differences?
- What discount pricing options are available?

Facilities

- What types of plants or manufacturing capabilities are available? Is there any capacity for the producing capability to increase? Determine the locations of facilities, as well as any logistics partnerships.

Personnel

- How large is the company and how does this compare to competitors in the industry? What human capital is key for their business to function?

Corporate and marketing strategies

- Overall corporate objectives, mission statements, and company news can be found on their website. You can review the company's annual reports for further information. Conference calls recorded quarterly are often taped and provide additional detail.

References

1. Brian O'Rourke, "What Is a SWOT Analysis?" *Entrepreneur,* last modified April 1, 2003, https://www.entrepreneur.com/article/61206.

2. Erica Olsen, "Internal and External Analysis," *OnStrategy,* last modified May 5, 2010, http://onstrategyhq.com/resources/internal-and-external-analysis.

6

TARGET MARKET PROFILE

MAIN IDEAS

- Use demographic and psychographics to predict consumer behavior.

- Discuss why this market is relevant and strong for your brand or product. Introduce VALS for consumer behavior and PRIZM for segmentation.

I n this section, you will learn how to develop a target market profile from the results of your situation analysis. The target market profile may or may not be the same as the consumer analysis. You may choose to select a part of the current segment versus continuing down the same path. Using this information, you should be able to tie directly into a specific segment focus. This segment focus will allow you get to narrow the focus that is manageable for the campaign: media mix selection and budgetary planning. The target market should be described in terms of their demographics and psychographics. Demographics will consist of age, income, employment, and gender. Psychographics will explore the lifestyles of the subject matters consumer behavior. There are two main resources with which you should be familiar: VALS for consumer behavior, and PRIZM for segmentation. Both of these resources will allow you to significantly narrow your target market.

The VALS framework, which is located on the Strategic Business Insights website, separates US adults into eight distinctive mentalities using a specific set of inner traits and key demographics that drive consumer behavior. These eight types will give you a framework for understanding consumers (Insights 2015).

The PRIZM segmentation system provides an interactive tool that lets you examine segment groups based on demographics and consumer behaviors (Nielsen 2015).

Once you have completed the market segmentation process, then you can proceed to selecting your target market. The target marketing process should begin with selecting segments identified from reviewing the VALS or PRIZM segments. Select a target market from the market segments you have identified. Next, choose the segment that is most important and specify it as the primary target market. Designate one or more segments as a target market. That group of segments you wish to attract and adapt its marketing activities toward. It is also wise to designate another set of segments as a secondary target market. In the event that there are alternative segments of importance if there are other important segments, designate them as secondary target markets. When defining your selected market segments, it is often wise to use a tool to help summarize the practicality of a potential market. After creating your profiles, compare and determine which market will present the best overall opportunity for your IMC plan. Use the matrix in Figure 6.0 to help define your target market.

Figure 6.0. Defining the Target Market

	CUSTOMERS	COMPETITION'S CUSTOMERS	NONUSERS
Demographics			
Age			
Gender			
Race/ethnicity			
Location/region			
Social class			
Income			
Education			
Behavioristic			
Product usage (light, medium, or heavy)			
Brand loyalty (loyal, disloyal)			
Psychographics			
Principle-oriented (yes or no)			
Status-oriented (yes or no)			
Action-oriented (yes or no)			
Benefits Sought			
Low price (yes or no)			
Quality (yes or no)			

References

1. "Competitive Analysis," *Entrepreneur,* accessed March 25, 2015, http://www.entrepreneur.com/encyclopedia/competitive-analysis.

2. "Market Segmentation," *Nielsen,* accessed April 2, 2015, https://segmentationsolutions.nielsen.com/mybestsegments/

3. "US Framework and VALS Types," *Strategic Business Insights,* accessed April 2, 2015, http://www.strategicbusinessinsights.com/vals/ustypes.shtml.

7

IMC OBJECTIVES AND STRATEGY

MAIN IDEAS

- Discuss the marketing, advertising, and IMC objectives you want to achieve with your campaign.

- Discuss why these objectives are reasonable and necessary for your product. Explain the role of each marketing communication for the campaign as a whole.

- Discuss why the strategies you chose are relevant to your target market.

IMC OBJECTIVES AND STRATEGY

I n this section, you want to begin developing a strategic approach towards what you actually want to accomplish. Review your situation analysis and look into the companies existing marketing plan for background information. Most companies will certainly have a mission statement and corporate objectives. Those corporate objectives provide direction for their marketing plan. Once you have established the strategy of the marketing plan, you can then analyze the gathered research and determine what IMC objectives you may want to achieve in the campaign. Consider the following key points when working to develop your concrete strategy.

1. Discuss the marketing, advertising, and IMC objectives you want to achieve with your IMC campaign.

    - Marketing objectives are often found in the company's marketing plan. Your marketing objectives should be specific and have measurable outcomes. Successful achievement of marketing objectives will depend on proper execution and coordination of the marketing mix.
    - Advertising objectives be able to attract the right buyers. In 1961, Russell Colley developed a model for setting advertising objectives and measuring the results of an ad campaign. According to the DAGMAR approach, an advertising goal involves a communications task that is specific and measurable. Planners who follow DAGMAR formulate objectives related to the following sequence:
      - **Awareness:** knowing the brand exists
      - **Comprehension:** knowing about the brand's benefits or attributes
      - **Conviction:** a favorable attitude toward the brand
      - **Action:** purchasing and using the brand

    When selecting your objectives, clearly review your situation analysis to determine which category is most suited for your IMC plan.

    - The IMC objectives are specific, measurable, and quantifiable statements regarding what each aspect of the IMC plan will accomplish. The objectives are based on what marketing communications will deliver specifically to the targeted audience. You must be able to articulate general marketing goals into communications goals and specific promotional objectives. When making these decisions, you can refer to the IMC Pyramid (Figure 7.1), which is a guide to setting objectives.

The IMC pyramid depicts the progression of communication outcomes that focus on mass audiences for products and services. This model usually is applied to advertising, and it tracks the stages of the consumer lifecycle from awareness to action.

The traditional order of the IMC pyramid is:

- Awareness
- Comprehension
- Conviction
- Desire
- Action

Awareness is considered to be the primary objective that familiarizes consumers with the brand, product and service. Comprehension, which is the next stage, aims to communicate enough information about the product so the audience understands the features, image, purpose, and brand position. Conviction occurs when enough information is communicated to persuade the audience to see the product's value. After the audience is convinced, they may experience desire and move towards taking action. The goal of marketing, advertising, and IMC objectives is to guide consumers through the multiple levels of the IMC pyramid.

2. After stating your marketing, advertising, and IMC objectives, make sure to provide detailed information about why they are reasonable and necessary for your product. This information will give the client a sense of appreciation and will provide an element of credibility to the plan.

3. Describe which marketing communications you will be using in the campaign. Explain the role of each marketing communication for the campaign as a whole. "See below for a list of different marketing communications"
   - Collateral Materials
   - Personal Selling
   - Public Relations
   - Sales Promotion
   - Product Advertising
   - Event Marketing
   - Interactive Marketing

4. Discuss your "Big Idea" (creative concept): major selling message/theme. The Big Idea is an attempt to communicate a brand, product, or concept to the general public by creating a strong message that pushes brand boundaries and resonates with the consumers. The big idea, which is the flash of insight, that takes place. The big idea is a bold, creative initiative that makes the audience stop, look, and listen.

5. Explain why the strategies you chose are relevant to your target market. Review and summarize your target market segments to ensure they will benefit from the strategy. This is where your campaign ideas come into play. What are you going to actually do to meet those IMC objectives? Think about strategies that will work well with the target market you selected. It is very important to use your situation analysis and all of your research to make these decisions.

The marketing, advertising, or IMC objectives may be expressed in terms of moving prospective consumers through the IMC pyramid, or they may be expressed in terms of generating inquiries, coupons, responses, or apparent changes.

Figure 7.0 DAGMAR Method

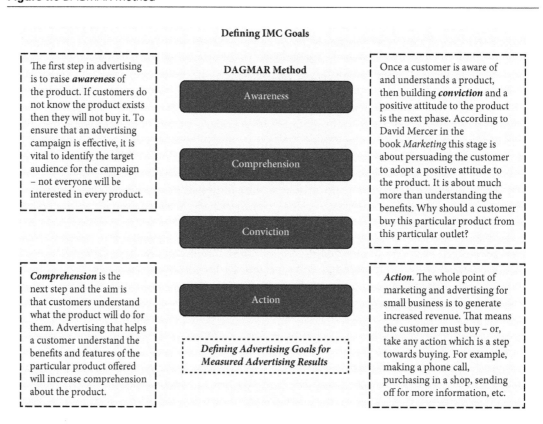

Defining IMC Goals

DAGMAR Method

Awareness

Comprehension

Conviction

Action

Defining Advertising Goals for Measured Advertising Results

The first step in advertising is to raise **awareness** of the product. If customers do not know the product exists then they will not buy it. To ensure that an advertising campaign is effective, it is vital to identify the target audience for the campaign – not everyone will be interested in every product.

Once a customer is aware of and understands a product, then building **conviction** and a positive attitude to the product is the next phase. According to David Mercer in the book *Marketing* this stage is about persuading the customer to adopt a positive attitude to the product. It is about much more than understanding the benefits. Why should a customer buy this particular product from this particular outlet?

Comprehension is the next step and the aim is that customers understand what the product will do for them. Advertising that helps a customer understand the benefits and features of the particular product offered will increase comprehension about the product.

Action. The whole point of marketing and advertising for small business is to generate increased revenue. That means the customer must buy – or, take any action which is a step towards buying. For example, making a phone call, purchasing in a shop, sending off for more information, etc.

Figure 7.1 IMC Pyramid

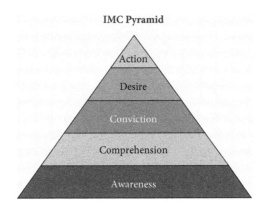

IMC Pyramid

- First section content
  - Summarize situational analysis and SWOT
  - Review target market segments
  - Itemize long- and short-term objectives
  - Re-state decisions regarding positioning and marketing mix
- Set objectives (using IMC Pyramid)
  - Review your long- and short-term objectives in conjunction with the IMC Pyramid in Figure 7.1. Determine which objectives are in line with the IMC pyramid.

References

1. "US Framework and VALS Types," *Strategic Business Insights,* accessed April 2, 2015, http://www.strategicbusinessinsights.com/vals/ustypes.shtml.

2. "Identifying Primary and Secondary Target Markets," *Full Brain Marketing,* last modified April 6, 2010, http://www.fullbrainmarketing.com/blog/identifying-primary-and-secondary-target-markets.

3. "Big Idea (marketing)," *Wikipedia,* last modified October 23, 2015, https://en.wikipedia.org/wiki/Big_Idea_(marketing).

4. William F. Arens, *Contemporary Advertising & Integrated Marketing Communications* (14 ed.) (New York: McGraw-Hill Education, 2013).

8

BUDGET

MAIN IDEAS

- Establish a total campaign budget and show the breakdown by all proposed marketing communications. Provide rationale for all of your recommendations.

- Discuss how you are going to split the budget between national media costs and regional (spot) campaign costs. Include a breakdown of the media cost by media mix and seasonality.

T he total size of the client's advertising budget can vary from a few thousand dollars to more than a million. Think about big companies—like Sprint and T-Mobile—that spend more than a billion dollars per year to promote their products. They expect these expenditures to deliver against their objectives.

The budget decision is very critical to clients campaign spending even if the monetary value is only a few hundred to a thousand dollars. It can be a strong successful event or failures depending on the amount of spend. Some often fail to associate the promotional spend as an expense instead of an investment.

In this section of your IMC plan, you want to focus on a total campaign budget. There many different ways to determine your budget. The most common measures used today are:

- A percentage of sales or profit
- Competitive threat
- Past successful campaigns

Normally, a media planner would determine the dollar amount to budget and how to allocate funds across various media channels. For example, the planner would determine how much to spend on print, TV, nontraditional, or supplemental media. The budget will also include the location or area spending.

The primary question at hand is how much you should recommend that your client spend on the marketing campaign. See below for alternative ways that many companies approach budget decisions.

- **Research:** Companies spend time and money running observations in different geographic areas determine an efficient way to spend their budget.
- **Market/Share:** Companies allocate dollars by percentage of total market spending or a desired share of the market.
- **Objective focus:** Companies define their objectives, then determine strategy and complete a cost estimate on how to execute the plan.
- **Sales percentage:** Companies determine the budget by allocating a combination of percentage of the previous year's sales and current forecasted sales.
- **Profits:** Companies allocate a percentage of the previous year's profits for their budget.
- **Unit of sale:** Companies set a specific dollar amount for each unit. This method is also called the case-rate method.
- **Competition:** Companies allocate dollars to match competitor's spend as a defensive mechanism.

After determining your actual budget, you will want to present a visual that demonstrates clearly how the funds will be allocated. Spreadsheets and graphs can show the plan's breakdown by all proposed marketing communications, and you will also discuss the justification for all recommendations. The advertising media cost will be split into national, regional, and local campaign cost. You should also include the breakdown of media cost by mix, and also consider seasonality when predicting cost.

Below, you will see marketing expenditures listed along with a monthly cost figure and a complete total for Q1. The figure also displays a breakdown of monthly marketing cost, company total sales, and marketing as a percentage of sales. A spreadsheet like this gives the client a clear understanding of marketing cost.

Figure 8.0. Budget Marketing Expenditure View

Q1 Marketing Expenditures	January	February	March	Q1 Totals
Online	$1,500.00	$1,000.00	$2,300.00	$4,800.00
Catalogs	$2,100.00	$1,500.00	$1,100.00	$4,700.00
Conventions	$1,111.00	$2,500.00	$2,300.00	$5,911.00
Trade shows	$1,200.00	$650.00	$555.00	$2,405.00
Print	$800.00	$1,150.00	$1,100.00	$3,050.00
Radio	$250.00	$890.00	$200.00	$1,340.00
Promotions	$250.00	$600.00	$200.00	$1,050.00
Publications	$2,300.00	$2,100.00	$1,900.00	$6,300.00
Sales training	$1,500.00	$2,340.00	$3,456.00	$7,296.00
Magazines	$600.00	$450.00	$200.00	$1,250.00
Total spent marketing in Q1	$11,611.00	$13,180.00	$13,311.00	$38,102.00
Company sales totals in Q1	$375,000.00	$400,000.00	$425,000.00	$1,200,000.00
Marketing as a % of sales	3.096%	3.295%	3.132%	3.175%

The bar chart shows an alternative way to visualize monthly marketing expenditures.

Figure 8.1. Budget Expenditure Chart by Month

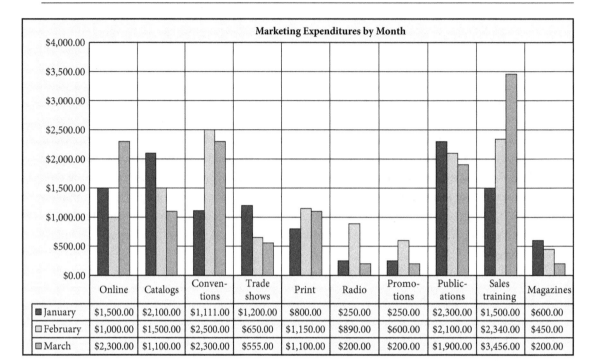

	Online	Catalogs	Conventions	Trade shows	Print	Radio	Promotions	Publications	Sales training	Magazines
■ January	$1,500.00	$2,100.00	$1,111.00	$1,200.00	$800.00	$250.00	$250.00	$2,300.00	$1,500.00	$600.00
□ February	$1,000.00	$1,500.00	$2,500.00	$650.00	$1,150.00	$890.00	$600.00	$2,100.00	$2,340.00	$450.00
▨ March	$2,300.00	$1,100.00	$2,300.00	$555.00	$1,100.00	$200.00	$200.00	$1,900.00	$3,456.00	$200.00

The chart below displays the percentage of marketing budget used for each type of marketing. The client can see a breakdown of marketing expenses by percentages.

Figure 8.2. Total marketing expenditures expenses by percentages

Total marketing expenditures expresses in %	100%
Online advertising	13%
Catalogs & brochures	12%
Conventions	16%
Trade shows	6%
Print advertising	8%
Radio	4%
Promotional items	3%
Publications	17%
Sales training	19%
Magazine	3%

The pie chart below also displays the percentage of the budget used for each type of marketing.

Figure 8.3. Pie Chart of Marketing Expenditures

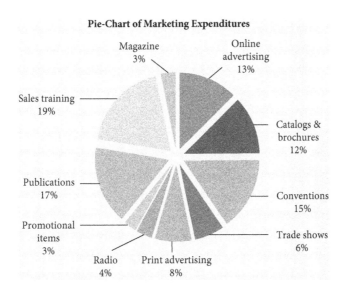

References

1. "Marketing Plan: Marketing Objectives and Strategies," *Small Business Notes*, accessed May 7th, 2015, http://www.smallbusinessnotes.com/starting-a-business/marketing-plan-marketing-objectives-and-strategies.html.

2. Gale Metzger, "Faith in Numbers: Lessons Old and New in Media Measurement," *Advertising Age*, last modified December 3, 2012, , http://adage.com/article/guest-columnists/faith-numbers-lessons-media-measurement/238558.

9

MEDIA OBJECTIVES

MAIN IDEAS

- Discuss how to select your media objectives for your media plan.

- Introduce basic components that are commonly used in media planning.

O ne of the biggest mistakes advertisers and their agencies make is failing to set specific objectives for their campaigns and plans. By failing to set objectives, advertisers have no evidence to determine whether or not their promotional efforts are successful. Your goal should be to set measurable objectives that guide planning and decisions, and can be used to evaluate campaign performance.

In this section, you will focus on stating your media objectives. To write and develop media objectives, you should start with the marketing objectives. The purpose of stating your media objectives is to translate your marketing and IMC strategies into goals that the media can accomplish.

Create an outline about what you anticipate the media plan will achieve. The media objectives are only designed to tell you what the media plan needs to achieve. You should not mention specific media selections in this section. Rather, media selections are normally covered in the strategy section.

When discussing media objectives, you must address at least two key components: **audience objectives,** which are specific types of consumers that advertisers will reach, and **message distribution objectives** that will define where, when and how often advertising will appear. It will be imperative that you gain a clear understanding of advertising weight and there elements weight, reach, frequency and continuity.

Guiding questions for developing media objectives:
- What is the target market?
- Where will you deliver the messages?
- When will you deliver the messages?
- What is the advertising weight, and over what period of time?

Figure 9.0. Marketing and Media Objective Examples

MARKETING OBJECTIVES	MEDIA OBJECTIVES
Increase awareness among target audience by 32%	Generate mass awareness among our target audience
Take back 8% share of sales from competition	Differentiate brand from the competition
Build a CRM database of 5000 new customers	Generate leads for more information

* Note: Media objectives can seem very similar to marketing objectives, although they are actually very different. Media objectives will focus only on what the media can achieve.

Sometimes media objectives will take on different shapes and forms to cover numerous subjects of the campaign. To ensure that media objectives are met, you will find the following basic components in most media plans:

- **Target audience:** Determine which consumers you are trying to reach. Your media objectives should consider the target audience for the brand. Make sure to review your marketing objectives and strategies to shape the appropriate target audience. If you have two target audiences, identify them as a primary or secondary segment.
- **Scheduling:** Write a schedule allocating advertising dollars across each month. Determine the appropriate strategies continuous, pulsing or flighting.
- **Reach/Frequency:** Determine the most effective level of reach and frequency. Explore your reach and frequency opportunities as part of your objectives to determine which months will receive high, medium, or levels of reach. Consider using the Ostrow Model to help determine the minimal level of frequency to be used.
- **Geographic coverage:** Determine in which geographic area(s) you will place your advertising. Consider the option for using top DMAs if there is a necessity for geographic importance.
- **Creative implications:** Determine if the creative strategy will have any consequences for your media plan.
- **Promotional support:** Get a strong understanding of all of your promotional efforts. Determine what will be necessary to support your promotional strategy.
- **Budget limitations:** Determine if your media budget is restricted in any way or if there are limitations that may impact the strategy.

Reference

1. Jack Neff, "P & G's Pritchard on Where Marketing, Media and Metrics are Going," *Advertising Age,* last modified March 16, 2015, http://adage.com/article/cmo-strategy/p-g-s-pritchard-marketing-metrics/297592.

10

MEDIA STRATEGY

MAIN IDEAS

- Decide on your communication media mix.

- Discuss your media of choice providing basis for recommendations.

- Determine appropriate scheduling, weight, reach and frequency

MEDIA STRATEGY

The media strategy discussed in chapter 10 will focus on your media selections. A media strategy explains how promoters will attain stated media objectives. In a media strategy, you should discuss three crucial decisions in detail: where to advertise (geography), when to advertise (timing), and which media categories to use (media mix).

Figure 10.0. Media Objectives & Media Strategies

MEDIA OBJECTIVES	MEDIA STRATEGIES
Generate mass awareness among target audience	Use mass media to build reach against males 18 -34
Differentiate brand from competition	Secure high–profile sponsorship with category exclusivity
Generate leads for more information	Use interactive media to elicit registration

* Note: See how your media objectives will translate into media strategies.

When making media mix decisions, you will consider both traditional and digital marketing media. There are many opportunities to acquaint consumers with the brand. Figure 10.1 outlines different forms of traditional and digital media.

Figure 10.1. Traditional vs. Digital Media

TRADITIONAL	DIGITAL
Print	Desktop website
TV	Mobile website
Radio	Mobile apps
Newspaper	Social media
OOH – Billboards	Digital signage
Magazines	Video
Brochures	Interactives

Figure 10.2 outlines specific advantages of various media platforms.

Figure 10.2. Media Platform Advantages

MEDIA PLATFORM	ADVANTAGES
Television	Reaches a mass audience in a single exposure.
Radio	Broadcast can be local, and therefore have a narrower target market focus.
Print publications	Reach target market geographically through newspaper and magazines.
Internet advertising	Using websites and email in the format of Two-way communication with limited targeted messaging and tracking capabilities.

(continued)

(continued)

MEDIA PLATFORM	ADVANTAGES
Direct mail	Allows for specialization, customization, and personalization.
OOH and Signage	High trafficking and visibility in geographically identified areas gains customer awareness.
Product placement	Brand creditability established by using influencers or the entertainment media.
Mobile	Two-way communication allows consumers on-the-go to stay informed.
Sponsorship	Paid resources to support events in exchange for branding opportunities.
Alternative media	Includes collateral materials, or placement on objects or clothing.

There are so many choices in media selection. It is important that you mix different media types for a quality IMC plan. It is critical that you understand the advantages of various media types.. When you are evaluating specific media vehicles, you should consider several factors. First, review your campaign objectives and strategies. Establish an understanding of your audience size and mediums that will include all of your cost efficiencies. Most often, you will have very different media categories that may affect your media objectives. You can segment these media options in three categories: point-of-purchase media, mass marketing media, and direct response media. Each media category choice will be determined by the objectives that are set. These three major categories empirically move the process from awareness to an interest in purchasing.

Figure 10.3. Media Selection Categories

CATEGORY	ACTIVITY	MEDIA
Point-of-purchase media	Conversion	Sampling, coupons, and price off promotions
Mass marketing media	Broad awareness, re-minder advertising, large audiences	Television, radio, newspaper, and magazines
Direct response media	Relationship building, persuasion, action	Direct mail, Internet and mobile advertising

After allocating media advertising to support the strategy, you must also allocate advertising by geography. Generally, most companies that sell nationally will consider one of three marketing approaches: national, spot, or combined approach. The national approach entails advertising in all markets. The spot approach requires being very selective with marketing efforts, and a combined approach will use both national and spot approaches.

There are two methods to perform geographic analyses. The Brand Development Index (BDI) focuses on measuring the brand's concentration by region. The Category Development Index (CDI) focuses on measuring the product category across all brands in a particular region.

After selecting your media mix, you must decide when and where to allocate your budget. There are three scheduling methods to consider: continuity, flight, or pulsing. In this area you can allocate spending across several months of the campaign. The continuity method will spread your funding evenly across the months of your campaign, thereby increasing brand exposure. This method will use a large portion of your budget. The flight method alternates advertising lightly in certain months, and advertising heavily in other months. The pulsing method involves both the continuity and flight methods and will result in a lower level of advertising across your campaign months. When selecting the right scheduling, you should consider seasonality, the purchasing cycle of consumers, consumer decision-making intervals, and consumption.

References

1. "Advertising Media Planning: A Primer," *Ad Media,* accessed July 8, 2015, http://www.admedia.org.
2. Kate Maddox, "Media Planners in High Demand," B to B No 13. (November 8, 2004): P.24.

11

MEDIA TACTICS

MAIN IDEAS

- This section will provide examples and follow the relevant format to show your media vehicle recommendations.

- This section will discuss how each medium needs to be justified. This chapter includes an example of a media flow chart.

MEDIA TACTICS

C hanges in the way people use, interrelate, and develop media have affected how an audience is measured and reached. Measuring traditional television audience and measuring online audiences are considerably different. Audience measures are supposed to look at how many people to identify who is actually in the audience. Typically listenership for radio, viewership for television, readership for newspaper and magazine measure the media.

After your media strategy has been established, the next task is to determine your media tactics. These tactics will focus on media vehicle selection, which includes reach, frequency, and Gross Rating Points (GRPs) Media reach aims to expose the target audience to the brand. Reach has three characteristics: percentage, accumulation of audience, and total number of audience exposed.

Figure 11.0 Reach Characteristics

CHARACTERISTICS	RESULTS
Percentage	With a target of 50 out of 50,000, the reach is 25,000
Accumulation of audience	Reach growing from 5% in the second week to 50% in the fourth week.
Total number of audience exposed	No duplication

(GRPs) are set up to measure the total amount of exposures. The difference between GRPs and reach is that GRPs count the total exposure, while reach only counts unique individuals that are exposed. Frequency, on the other hand, measures the recurrence of the exposure.

Remember that your client or boss wants you to help the company sell more products. In this IMC plan, you will provide many charts, tables, and other visualizations that the client may or may not be able to comprehend. Providing your client with a flowchart can help. The flowchart provides at-a-glance information regarding when your proposed ads will run, in which media vehicles, at what cost, and to what effects (reach and frequency). See Figure 11.1 for a flowchart sample. There are many different ways of creating a media flowchart, including drawing one yourself, using a computer program, or using media flowchart software.

Figure 11.1. Media Flowchart

Campaign
ESH Enterprises Advertising
3 Media Flowchart

MEDIA	2015		2016	Net Cost
	JUL AUG SEP OCT NOV DEC		JAN FEB MAR APR MAY JUN	
TELEVISION				$77,000
CBS	10 GRP's	10 GRP's	10 GRP's	$22,000
PRINT				
Fortune (1/2 page ad)	1.2MM Circulation	1.2MM Circulation	1.2MM Circulation	$14,000
Sports Illustrated (1 page ad)	125,000 Circ.	125,000 Circ.	125,000 Circ. 125,000 Circ.	$15,000
RADIO				
Sirius	2 TRP's	2 TRP's	2 TRP's	$3,000
DIGITAL				
Twitter	100,000 Impressions	100,000 Impressions	100,000 Impressions	$11,000
Facebook	75,000 Impressions	75,000 Impressions	75,000 Impressions	$12,000
	EXAMPLE EXAMPLE EXAMPLE		EXAMPLE EXAMPLE EXAMPLE	
Totals				$77,000

In this section of your IMC plan you will discuss how each medium will be justified and substantiated. Show your recommendation for each medium selected. Complete your media flow chart with all necessary information that includes qualitative and quantitative characteristics: GRPs, Reach/Frequency achieved, total cost of each media described. The media flow chart shows media being used. Messaging insertion timing and cost of the media.

Reference

1.   "Advertising Media Planning: A Primer," *Ad Media*, accessed July 19, 2015, http://www.admedia.org.

12

THE IMC EVALUATION

MAIN IDEAS

- Discuss the effectiveness of IMC planning and what to measure.

- Discuss the effectiveness of IMC plan and how to measure.

THE IMC EVALUATION

The IMC plan must have a degree of accountability for several reasons. Companies that invest in advertising expect a return on their investment. Measuring outcomes is an integral part of the IMC plan, and provides clients with a source of guarantee, and a way to adjust the campaign. It is important, therefore, to identify which measures are most relevant to the effectiveness IMC plan.

What are some of the key things we should be measuring? Start with your media flowchart to examine execution of scheduled media placements. Look at the metrics to determine if there is a discrepancy. Make sure the ads appear in the media vehicles.

The best way to measure effectives is to determine the exposures of various media vehicles. You should also evaluate whether the planned target audiences were reached in the planned time period.

The DAGMAR method is a standardized industry tool used to measure advertising results. Components of the DAGMAR method include:

- **Brand awareness:** Determining which segments of the target market audience are aware of the brand.
- **Comprehension:** Making sure the target audience has a clear understanding of the brand.
- **Conviction:** Does the target audience have a desire for the brand, and are they convinced this is the right brand for them?
- **Action:** The target audience has purchased or will purchase the brand.

Some of the best methods for measuring the effectiveness of your IMC plan include surveys, feedback, tracking, and observation.

- **Surveys:** Sampling the target market during various phases of a campaign.
- **Feedback:** Collecting information like size of the audience, email addresses, and brand cards to determine the effectiveness of the campaign.
- **Tracking:** Using digital means to accumulate reports from the target market about the effectiveness of the campaign. Tracking can also include audience interaction.
- **Observation:** Depending on the media strategy, you will have the opportunity to visualize the target audience's activities. Observing these activities in motion—whether at an event or at a mall—allows you to capture a significant amount of data.

Figure 12.0. Defining IMC Goals with DAGMAR

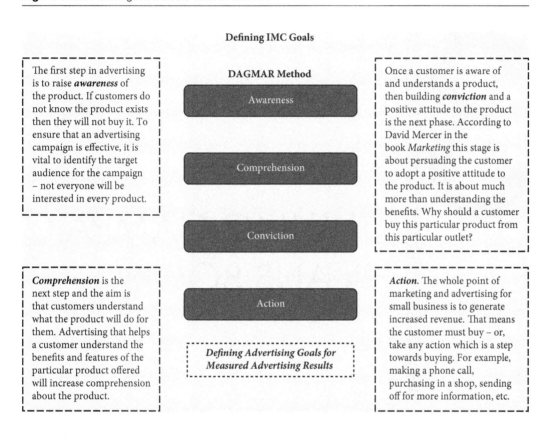

Defining IMC Goals

DAGMAR Method

The first step in advertising is to raise *awareness* of the product. If customers do not know the product exists then they will not buy it. To ensure that an advertising campaign is effective, it is vital to identify the target audience for the campaign – not everyone will be interested in every product.

Once a customer is aware of and understands a product, then building *conviction* and a positive attitude to the product is the next phase. According to David Mercer in the book *Marketing* this stage is about persuading the customer to adopt a positive attitude to the product. It is about much more than understanding the benefits. Why should a customer buy this particular product from this particular outlet?

Comprehension is the next step and the aim is that customers understand what the product will do for them. Advertising that helps a customer understand the benefits and features of the particular product offered will increase comprehension about the product.

Action. The whole point of marketing and advertising for small business is to generate increased revenue. That means the customer must buy – or, take any action which is a step towards buying. For example, making a phone call, purchasing in a shop, sending off for more information, etc.

Awareness

Comprehension

Conviction

Action

Defining Advertising Goals for Measured Advertising Results

References

1.   "Dagmar," *Investopedia*, accessed January 25, 2015, http://www.investopedia.com/terms/d/dagmar.asp.

2.   "Evaluation Metrics," *Ad Media,* accessed February 3, 2015, http://www.admedia.org.

3.   Becca Goldstein, March 23, 2015, Adweek, Use this model to Evaluate Your Omnichannel Strategy, accessed March 25th, 2015, http://www.adweek.com/brandshare/neustar

13

THE IMC CAMPAIGN PLANS BOOK

MAIN IDEAS

- This should be a formal "report" formatted with a title page, table of contents, and sources.

- Consider this report as a professional document being provided to the client or your boss. Discuss the importance of this document and how it will sell the campaign.

T he following pages provide a sample of an integrated marketing communications plan for the Doritos brand. Normally in my class I go through the following IMC plan to give students examples of each section with actual content that I have researched. However, the content is not as important in the sample as an understanding of the type of information that goes into each section.

TITLE PAGE: SAMPLE – INTEGRATED MARKETING COMMUNICATION PLAN FOR DORITOS

by **Eric Harvey**

TABLE OF CONTENTS

- Company Analysis
- Environmental Analysis
- Product Analysis
- Consumer Analysis
- Competitive Analysis
- SWOT Analysis
- Analysis of Research
- Target Market Profile
- Objectives and Strategies
- Campaign Objectives
- Advertising Strategy
- Future Goals from Campaign
- Budget
- Media Objectives
- Primary Target Market
- Creative Implications
- Budget Limitations
- Strategy
- Media Mix
- Scheduling
- Media Tactics: Specific Vehicle Recommendation
- Media Flow Chart
- Television
- Radio
- Digital
- Social Media
- Works Cited

Company Analysis

In 1932, Elmer Doolin founded the Frito Company in San Antonio, Texas, and began making Fritos corn chips. In 1938, Herman Lay bought the company, and changed the name to H.W. Lay & Company. In 1961, the H.W. Lay & Company and Frito Company merged to form the company now known as Frito-Lay, Inc. In 1965, Frito-Lay merged with PepsiCo to form a snack and beverage powerhouse. In 1966, Frito-Lay invented a new chip they called "Doritos." Frito-Lay's philosophy is to create a chip that makes people want to come back for more. The company offers a variety of different flavors to satisfy a variety of consumer's desires. Frito-Lay utilizes contests and campaigns to gain a better understanding of the flavors that their consumers desire. These contests and campaigns are successful primarily because the company utilizes an existing consumer base.

Frito-Lay's mission statement reads, "In order to make the best snacks on earth, we need to protect the earth. So we've committed to making sustainable products in four ways." Because the Doritos brand revolves around boldness, the Doritos mission statement is a little different. It reads, "If you're up to the challenge, grab a bag of DORITOS® tortilla chips and get ready to make some memories you won't soon forget. It's a bold experience in snacking and beyond."

The Doritos brand has been most successful in the Northwest. Doritos is Frito-Lay's second best-seller after Lay's potato chips. In 1993, Doritos was declared America's favorite snack food. Their annual sales were approximately $1.3 billion. Frito-Lay is the world's largest seller in snack foods. They control nearly thirty percent of the world's market in snack chips, and sixty percent of the US market. Frito-Lay has five major incomes with sales of $1 billion or more each: Lays, Doritos, Cheetos, Ruffles, and Tostitos. Frito-Lay makes up about two-thirds of PepsiCo's profits, and 10.2% of all salty snacks sold in the United States are Doritos chips.

Environmental Analysis

Owned by parent company Frito-Lay, Doritos has become one of the largest snack companies in the United States through the brand's effective use of marketing strategies and tactics. Doritos understands that to be successful in both the domestic and global market they must develop an understanding of the environmental factors around them that shape the profitability of Doritos. The environmental factors most relevant to the success of Doritos include an understanding of demographics, global economic interdependence, ethics, and technology.

By knowing their customers' demographics, Doritos is able to incorporate marketing strategies effectively. As a brand of Frito-Lay and PepsiCo, Doritos has relatively easy access to marketing and advertising funds that are used to bring in and retain customers. For example, Doritos teaming up with Taco Bell to create the mouthwatering Doritos Locos Tacos was a prime demonstration of both companies understanding their desired millennial target markets, and reaching them with a product that was a hit on social media.

Global economic interdependence is a concept companies understand more and more each day. With resources becoming more globally linked and products becoming more globally available, companies like Doritos need to recognize the competitive advantage of distributing products worldwide, and gaining increased global brand awareness. Before Doritos entered the Japanese market, the company analyzed the environmental factors of the Japanese market and determined that Japanese consumers have different taste preferences. A number of new flavors were created and added to Doritos' Japanese product line. With flavors such as coconut curry, tuna mayo, and wasabi mayo, the product line was a huge success and further proof that proper market research leads to increased profits.

PepsiCo is a forerunner of conducting responsible business practices in all of its branches, including Doritos. Within each company, employees must annually be re-certified in ethics courses and must listen to managers present about ethics and social responsibility. To further promote good business ethics, Frito-Lay has a "zero-landfill" initiative in which they encourage recycling for all brands packaged under Frito-Lay—including Doritos—by promising to give $0.02 for each recycled bag to a school or non-profit organization of the consumer's choice. Because of this recycling program—combined with the use of renewable energy sources such as solar power, recycled steam and heat, and bio-fuels—Frito-Lay estimates that it will use 45% less energy per chip bag by the year 2017.

From a technological standpoint, Doritos has incorporated the latest and greatest technologies to help aid online marketing and product promotions for the Doritos product line. One popular promotion is Doritos' customer-made commercials. The contest is typically run early in the year (around the time of the Super Bowl) and the winners get to see their Doritos commercial aired for the rest of the year. However, funny commercials are not the only way Doritos wants to interact with their customers. Under each product line, product information such as price and nutritional values can be found.

Whether Doritos is trying to satisfy their domestic or global marketing mix, the brand is keen on analyzing both internal and external environmental factors that contribute to their bottom line. To continue being a market leader and maintaining profitability, Doritos must continue to conduct proper market research that takes into account environmental factors such as demographics, the global economy, good business ethics, and technology usage.

Product Analysis

"Little Gold Thing"—now known as Doritos—made their first debut at the Casa de Fritos restaurant in Disneyland. Starting off with a simple taco seasoning, they were not the same Doritos we know and love today. Frito-Lay discovered the success of the "Little Gold Thing" and immediately made a deal to begin producing the chip for distribution. Frito-Lay began producing the chip in 1964, and the snack was released in 1966 for immediate sales. Doritos were the first tortilla chip to be launched nationally in the United States—a snack market traditionally dominated by potato chips and pretzels.

Today there are a variety of Doritos flavors—ranging from Cool Ranch to Sweet and Spicy Chili—that make the brand stand out as a bold, flavorful snack. One thing that all of the flavors have in common are the experience that eating Doritos provides the consumer. During an interview with Business Insider in 2012, PepsiCo Chief Marketing Officer Ram Krishnan explained the Dorito experience as follows: "Frito-Lay has to provide a product experience that you can't get anywhere else. It's not just the product itself—it's everything from start to finish. The bag, for instance, screams bright orange cheese. When you take the product out of the bag, your hand gets all cheesy. After taking a bite, the flavor hits your tongue first, and at the end, it gives you a smooth cheese feel. And, of course, once you're done, you have to lick the cheese off of your fingers." Doritos provides a unique snacking experience for consumers.

The Doritos brand focuses on being bold and breaking outside of the norm. Consumers who eat Doritos know that they have a voice and the brand urges them to use it. Doritos shows consumers that they matter through participatory marketing efforts. A few of the brand's advertising campaigns—such as Crash the Super Bowl—reflect these efforts.

The Doritos product life cycle is at maturity. Sales are growing at slow rates and finally stabilizing. However, products are still being differentiated and price wars and sales promotions are becoming more common. In turn, weaker brands are exiting the category.

Frito-Lay is a large player in the salty snack category. As a company, Frito Lay's market share is 35% of the category and is ranked first overall in the category (Market Share Reporter, 2013). In the category of tortilla and tostada chips, Doritos is ranked first—above brands such as Tostitos and Mission—and has a market share of 39.11%.

Doritos has always gone above and beyond with their advertising campaigns in order to make sure that consumers are blown away by the boldness of the product. A few of the brand's past advertising campaigns are discussed below. that were found in the Encyclopedia for Major Marketing Campaigns.

In 1966, Doritos debuted their "Get A Life" campaign. Unlike other Doritos campaigns, this advertising had a very broad target market: 12-34 year olds. With this campaign, Doritos sent the message that Doritos was "Everybody's Snack."

In 1977, Doritos changed methods and focused on a more narrow target market. Their "The Loudest Taste on Earth" campaign was geared towards 16–21 year olds, also known as "Generation X-ers." This target market enjoyed alternative music and grew up watching rock videos on MTV, which is why Doritos began to market themselves as a brand that allows consumers to break outside of the norm. With this campaign, Doritos stressed the loud crunch of the product, which is typically frowned upon in social settings. "The Loudest Taste on Earth" played on the joy of "allowed to be loud" and appealed to young people that liked to challenge the rules of etiquette. With twenty TV spots aired, Doritos conveyed an attitude of unrestrained exhilaration.

In 2013, Doritos launched their first global campaign: "For the Bold." The idea behind the campaign was to focus on international sales and make the Doritos brand more consistent across the thirty-seven different countries in which the chips are sold. In addition to updating their packaging and logo, Doritos unveiled TV spots, concert promotions, and a social media campaign. When asked about the campaign, Chief Marketing Officer Ram Krishnan stated, "With the rise of social media and technology, our world is smaller and more connected than ever before. We have found that our consumers across the world share very similar passions and interests, but until now may not have had a consistent way of speaking about the Doritos brand. The campaign is our way of connecting these fans worldwide, as we now provide a consistent storyline, and look and feel from the Doritos brand (Ad Age, 2013)."

One of Doritos' current advertising campaigns is "Crash The Super Bowl." This event provides a way for Doritos to interact with their consumers. In the fall of 2006, Frito-Lay decided to go against the norm of Super Bowl advertisements by not airing standard agency-made ads, but rather inviting their consumers to create their own Doritos advertisements. The finalists received $25,000 and the winner (chosen by online votes) received $1,000,000 and had their advertisement aired during the Super Bowl. Participatory marketing efforts not only allow the consumer to feel more connected to the brand, but also provide the brand with thousands of free ads.

Doritos has done it all when it comes to advertising. In addition to large campaigns, the brand advertises on a daily basis using billboards, social media, point-of-purchase displays at grocery and convenience stores, internet advertisements, and pairing with other brands such as Taco Bell and the film *Transformers*. The pairing between Taco Bell and Doritos to create the Doritos Locos Tacos resulted in $1 billion in sales for Taco Bell. In 2009 Ad Week reported that "The snacks group spent $146 million advertising brands like Doritos and Cheetos in 2008, and $118 million through July of this year, excluding online, per Nielsen. Additionally, under Mukherjee's leadership, Frito-Lay brands have garnered several industry-coveted awards, including two Cannes gold Lions, the Grand Ogilvy Award and a gold Effie Award."

Doritos has seen extraordinary responses to their marketing efforts. In 1977, Doritos' "Loudest Taste on Earth" campaign grew the brand's sales from $9.7 billion to $10.4 billion. The "Crash the Super Bowl" campaign is increasing all measures of pass-along value, online contest currency, media value, brand equity, and sales.

In 1977 Doritos changed their methods and focused on a more narrow target market. Their "The Loudest Taste on Earth" campaign was geared towards 16-21 year olds, also known as Generation X-ers. This target market enjoyed alternative music and grew up watching rock videos on MTV, which is why Doritos began to market themselves as a brand that will allow you to break outside of the norm. With this campaign, Doritos stressed the loud crunch the product made when eaten, which is typically frowned upon in social settings. "The Loudest Taste on Earth" played on the joy of "allowed to be loud" and appealed to young people that like to challenge the rules of etiquette. With 20 TV spots being aired, Doritos conveyed an attitude of unrestrained exhilaration.

In 2013 Doritos launched their first global campaign, "For the Bold". The idea behind the campaign was to focus on international sales and make the Doritos brand more consistent across the 37 different countries that they are sold in. Besides updating the packaging and logo, there were TV spots, concert promotions, and a social media campaign. Ad Age asked Ram Krishnan, the Chief Marketing Officer of Frito Lay, to talk about the campaign and he stated: "With the rise of social media and technology, our world is smaller and more connected than ever before," Mr. Krishnan said. "We have found that our consumers across the world share very similar passions and interests, but until now may not have had a consistent way of speaking about the Doritos brand. The campaign is our way of connecting these fans worldwide, as we now provide a consistent storyline, and look and feel from the Doritos brand (Ad Age, 2013)."

Currently for their advertising campaigns, Doritos takes place in Crash The Super Bowl. This event was created as a way for Doritos to interact with their consumers. In Fall 2006 Frito Lay decided to go against the norm of Super Bowl advertisements by not airing the standard agency-made ads, but instead invite their consumers to create their own Doritos advertisements. The finalists received $25,000 and the winner (chosen by online votes) had an advertisement in the Super Bowl and won a million dollars. Doritos participatory marketing efforts not only allow the consumer to feel more connected to the brand, but when it is all said and done they have over 25,000 ads that they are able to use that consumers have submitted without having to spend a dime on advertising.

Doritos has done it all when it comes to advertising. Besides their large campaigns, they advertise on a day-to-day basis using billboards, social media, point of purchase displays at grocery and convenience stores, Internet advertisements, promotions by pairing with large names, such as Taco Bell and Transformers the movie. The pairing between Taco Bell and Doritos to create the Doritos Locos Tacos resulted in $1 billion in sales for Taco Bell. In 2009 Ad Week reported: "The snacks group spent $146 million advertising brands like Doritos and Cheetos in 2008, and $118 million through July of this year, excluding online, per Nielsen. Additionally, under Mukherjee's leadership, Frito-Lay brands have garnered several industry-coveted awards, including two Cannes gold Lions, the Grand Ogilvy Award and a gold Effie Award."

Doritos has seen an extraordinary response to their marketing efforts. Going back in time to 1977 for their "Loudest Taste on Earth" campaign Doritos grew their sales from $9.7 billion to $10.4 billion. Coming back to present day, their 'Crash the Super Bowl' advertising efforts are increasing all measures of pass-along value, online contest currency, media value, brand equity and sales.

Consumer Analysis

Doritos consumers are lively, adventurous people, and Doritos delivers a chip suited for this lifestyle. Doritos are a bold, full-flavored chip for someone who is ready for this lifestyle and can is read for more. The real cheese flavor that of Doritos is one reason the chips have such a loyal following.

(americasgreatestbrands.com)

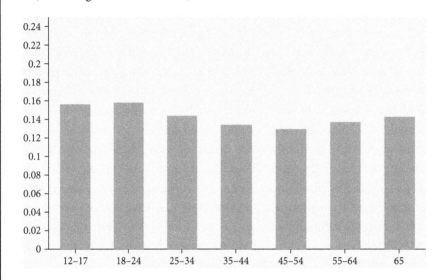

Figure 13.0. Doritos Demographic

Doritos' consumers consist primarily of 18–24 year olds, who make up 15.8% of the Doritos market as a whole. While this may seem surprising to some, this age bracket includes college students who have a larger salty snack budget than other consumers due to diet and lifestyle choices. The next largest consumer segment consists of 12–17 year olds, who make up 15.6% of the Doritos market. Their disposable income and/or allowances allows them to purchase salty snacks and beverages. This also then carries on into the next demographic where it expands even more (lexicalist.com).

In terms of gender, males make up 49.7% of the Doritos market and females make up 50.3%. This may seem surprising, but the boldness and cheese flavor of Doritos appeal to both sexes. Interestingly, Doritos does not include many women in their advertisements. This suggests the brand's effort to attract male consumers by appealing to male humor. (lexicalist.com).

The geographic areas in which Doritos performs best are surprising. At first glance, there is no real pattern to Doritos' geographic successes. Coastal areas tend to have lower sales of Doritos. The five most profitable states for Doritos are Alabama, Iowa, Kentucky, Nebraska, and Rhode Island.

Doritos fans are very loyal and have good reason to be so. Flavors range from the traditional Nacho Cheese and Cool Ranch to the new Doritos Dinamita—small rolled chips instead of the traditional triangular cut. The brand also released Doritos Jacked, and marketed these chips as having even more of an extreme flavor than original Doritos.

Consumers now have more power with the Doritos brand than ever, especially when it comes to advertising. As of 2006, the brand has given more airtime to consumer-made commercials. Who else is better equipped to make commercials? 2.4% 2.5% 2.9% 2.5% 2.9%

Doritos has more than 14 Doritos commercials than their target audience? This makes the best commercials because the target knows what the other people like them want to see and what will help them remember Doritos the next time they buy a salty snack.

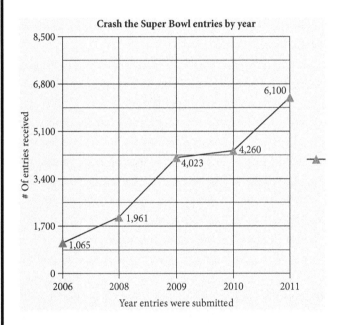

Figure 13.1. 2006 Commercial Entries

With all the submissions it is impossible to say that the prior tactics aren't working. Since 2006, Doritos has received an increasing number of commercial entries. This increase demonstrates both a consumer interest in advertising, as well as consumer pride and loyalty more generally.

Competitive Analysis

Doritos has many competitors, with some being more aggressive than others. The brand's three biggest competitors in the snack food industry are Lays, Cheez-It, and Pringles. Even though Lays is a parent company of Doritos, they are still an aggressive competitor.

Cheez-It crackers are not chips, but the brand is still in the competitive snack food industry. According to the Market Share Reporter, Cheez-It owns 13.69% of the snack food market. In 2013, Cheez-It had a whopping $590.7 million in sales (Statista). Cheez-It has made major marketing efforts in the past few years, mainly through commercials. Unlike Doritos and most other snack foods, Cheez-It benefits from being a kosher snack, and having zero grams of trans fat. This benefits their brand because most snack foods don't offer a snack that has 0 grams of trans fat or that are kosher certified. The Cheez-It brand has used funny commercials to catch the attention of their consumers. They have multiple commercials that all have some sort of humor in them starring the aged cheese. Cheez-Itz has had really successful advertisements. Some Cheez-It flavors, however, have not appealed to consumers and therefore have not been successful or profitable.

Like Doritos, the Pringles brand includes many flavors. Their wide flavor variety makes Pringles one of Dorito's main competitors. According to the Market Share Reporter, Pringles owns 9.05% of the snack food market. When the Kellogg Company bought Pringles from Procter & Gamble, the Pringles brand was making $1.5 billion in sales every year. The Pringles brand also offers a healthier alternative to its original flavor. Reduced fat Pringles contain five grams of fat per serving, compared to nine grams of fat for the original flavor. Doritos, on the other hand, is disadvantaged because the brand does not offer any healthier alternatives. Pringles is position by their product attribute just like Dorito's is, meaning they are compared by their price and or quality. Ever since the Kellogg Company purchased the Pringles brand, they have invested in little to no advertising for their product. When I was younger, I remember frequently seeing Pringles commercials and begging my mom to buy Pringles on her next trip to the grocery store. In the past, Pringles advertisements have helped the brand. Television ads for Pringles often showed people having a good time and were therefore appealing to consumers. Even without television ads and extra advertising spending, the brand is still successful. Personalization attempts have not worked well for the Pringles brand. The company allows consumers to submit flavor ideas, but the flavors are so odd that nobody wanted to buy them.

Even though Lays is Dorito's parent company, they are still an active competitor for Doritos. According to the Market Share Reporter, Lays owns 29.72% of the snack food market. "Lay's original flavor was just shy of collection $1.6 billion in sales," according to Statista. Lays also offers slightly healthier alternatives for its consumers. The brand produces baked chips, which are supposedly healthier than the original flavors and chips. These healthier options, benefit the Lays brand because Doritos does not offer any healthier options. As the market leader, Lays has a good position in the market and has a competitive advantage over most snack foods. Unlike in the past, Lays has not recently made many television ads. Like Cheez-It, the Lays brand also tries to appeal to customers through humor. Lays wants to catch the consumer's attention and make them laugh so they will end up buying their product. Another advantage for Lays is being a part of Frito-Lay and PepsiCo. These are well-known companies with many loyal consumers. which leads to the consumers continuing to by their products and revenue continues to come in for the company.

One approach that has not worked well for Lays is positioning themselves as a healthy brand. They only offer a few flavors in the baked style, and they do not taste the same as the original chips. As far as shelf position goes for these brands, they are all the same. Typically, each brand is located in the chip aisle, but occasionally one of the three brands is displayed at the end of an aisle.

Doritos	Pringles
S : Strong Global Brand Advertising Excellent Distribution and Branding W: Other Snack Segments Sales in emerging markets O : New Flavors International Markets Celebrity Endorsements T : Changing Diet Trends Pringles	S : Innovation Consistent Formulas W: Different Flavors in different countries Advertisement O : Odd flavors Pringles Prints Healthy Alternatives T : Sales in other countries 6% decline in operating profit in 2013
Lays	**Cheeze-itz**
S : Loyal Customers Customer engagement W: Advertising Unhealthy O : Chocolate covered potato chips Gluten-free alternative T : Doritos Avoidance of high fat content products	S : Cracker and Chip industry Advertising W: Customer involvement Web-site O : Children snack Cheese puff machine T : Cheese nips, Doritos, Cheetos At home Gluten-free cheeze-it recipe

Figure 13.2. SWOT Analysis

<table>
<tr><td colspan="2">

Doritos

S : Strong Global Brand
    Advertising
    Excellent Distribution and Branding
W: Other Snack Segments
    Sales in emerging markets
O : New Flavors
    International Markets
    Celebrity Endorsements
T : Changing Diet Trends
    Pringles

</td><td>

Pringles

S : Innovation
    Consistent Formulas
W: Different Flavors in different countries
    Advertisement
O : Odd flavors
    Pringles Prints
    Healthy Alternatives
T : Sales in other countries
    6% decline in operating profit in 2013

</td></tr>
<tr><td>

Lays

S : Loyal Customers
    Customer engagement
W: Advertising
    Unhealthy
O : Chocolate covered potato chips
    Gluten-free alternative
T : Doritos
    Avoidance of high fat content products

</td><td>

Cheeze-itz

S : Cracker and Chip industry
    Advertising
W: Customer involvement
    Web-site
O : Children snack
    Cheese puff machine
T : Cheese nips, Doritos, Cheetos
    At home Gluten-free cheeze-it recipe

</td></tr>
</table>

Fig. 13.2 SWOT Analysis (repeated)

Doritos has strong brand equity, because consumers see them as a trustworthy brand. This leads to consumers being loyal to Doritos and coming back for more of their products. I think that they really have the upper hand because they are part of Frito-Lays and PepsiCo., which are two proven brands. Their quality is much better than any generic alternative, even if it is a couple dollars more, most consumers are willing to pay it for that quality. Also, their advertisements have also led them to have strong brand equity.

Strengths

The largest strength for the Doritos brand is distinct taste. The brand also excels in advertising, especially consumer-generated advertising. It allow for consumer not only to feel pride in their own world and show it off but there are so many submissions and there are bound to be great ones so then they get more than they ever could with advertising campaign.

Another strength of the Doritos brand is its dominance of the flavored, cheese-coated tortilla chip market. The brand has been able to stifle competitors and maintain its larger market share.

Weaknesses

Doritos is avoiding other snack segments. The brand attempts to be better than their main competitors, which are Lays, Cheez-It, and Pringles. Compared to competitors, Doritos advertisements do not always reach the primary target market effectively. Another weakness of the Doritos brand is that they offer no healthier snacking alternative in a society that increasingly values healthy eating.. Many companies have been frowned upon for not have a selection of healthy alternatives. Being seen as an unhealthy snack and not having many alternatives hurts Doritos. The brand offers some reduced-fat chips, but these options are still not a very healthy choice when comparing them to alternative snacks. The Doritos brand needs to focus more on sales in emerging markets. They are doing well in their current market, but could increase sales by expanding into other markets.

Opportunities

Expanding their product portfolio will always be a positive opportunity for Doritos. People are constantly changing and new flavors are always trending. Being able to capitalize on these trends will give Doritos an upper hand in the market. Doritos needs to make an effort to expand their product portfolio not only in the United States, but also in international markets. Another opportunity for the Doritos brand is to gain increased market share in international markets through advertisements and marketing efforts. Celebrity endorsements provide one potential method for increasing market share. Currently, Doritos is capitalizing on participatory marketing, but pairing the Doritos name with well-known celebrities would increase brand recognition even more.

Threats

There are three noteworthy threats to the Doritos brand and company: the rivalry between Doritos and other Frito-Lay brand products, competition from outside firms, and changing dietary trends in western markets (most notably the United States). Together, these threats could destroy the Doritos brand in a matter of months, but as a market leader, Doritos remains ahead of the game by playing on its proven strengths.

Being under Parent Company Frito-lays, and Grandparent Company Pepsico, Doritos must compete horizontally essentially with itself. With multiple snack brands under its wing, Doritos is fighting to be the consumer's number one choice at the vending machine. Although Frito-Lay brands are in a small competition amongst themselves, together they fight a bigger battle for market share against other successful chip companies such as Pringles.

The biggest threat to Doritos—as well as to the snack industry at large—is the shift toward more healthy food options. Since the threat of global warming became a worldwide concern, individuals are reshaping their lifestyle choices and—more importantly—their diets. Over the past few years, the snack industry and other large industries have been on a steady decline in the US market. To combat the issue of changing diet trends, Doritos can do two things: change their product line and reposition themselves as a healthier snack alternative, or expand to foreign markets where the health trend has yet to strike.

Analysis of Research

We collected the data by dividing and allocating tasks to our specific group members. Because this project directly relates to our majors, we took our roles in our House Cat Marketing

Research firm very seriously. We spent a large amount of time doing research for this project and ended up with a collection of many valuable sources. We began our search very basically with a Google search to see all of our options and the various routes we could take with our product. After allocating tasks, we were each in charge of researching our individual parts for the Integrated Marketing Communication plan. Many of our meetings took place at the library, in an open group setting that allowed for discussion and building of ideas using all of our individual research. After we worked individually on our assigned parts, we met virtually every day to keep each other informed on our progress with the report.

The findings of our research helped us tremendously with our IMC plan. We learned a lot about Doritos that we did not know previously. We learned that Doritos is a Frito-Lay brand owned by PepsiCo, Inc. We learned about the unique history of Doritos, the brand's broad and specific competitors, how the brand does business on a large scale, and the SWOT analysis of the company. All of our research allowed us to understand how Doritos works as a whole.

One powerful insight we have considered is why people choose Doritos over other snacks. There are many snack foods to choose from, but we have narrowed down a few reasons why people choose Doritos over alternative snacks. Consumers want a tasty and easily accessible snack, but they are also considering other factors when making their snack decisions.

One strength of the Doritos brand is its product lineup of bold flavors. While researching, we learned that some countries have their own specific flavors that reflect their culture. For example, the Japanese market includes flavors like smoked bacon and cheese avocado that are not available in the US market. It is also interesting to note that flavor names change from country to country. In Iceland, for example, the Cool Ranch flavor is called Cool American. There are over thirty different Doritos flavors worldwide. They have even started developing a Dorito-flavored Mountain Dew.

Another interesting fact about Doritos is that the chips were the first product ever advertised in space. Also, Doritos is not just an invented name. The brand's name comes from the Spanish word *doradito*, meaning "little golden thing." The inventor of Doritos even had the chips sprinkled in his grave..

All of the information we gained from our research had the potential to help our IMC campaign, giving us a variety of creative routes to take. We can pride ourselves on factual information that is accessible to anyone that would want to see it. We could also pride ourselves on our creative ideas presented by each group member. In our campaign, we had the option to inform people that there is a flavor for every person, but it's up to "you" to find yours. Another idea that we discussed as a group was the theme of road trip.

Target Market Profile

For our Doritos campaign we have identified three distinct target markets. The primary target market is the young, educated, and hormonally imbalanced 18–24 year old demographic. The secondary target market is mothers or other parents who purchase Doritos mainly for their children to consume as a snack. The third target market is the everyday vending machine Doritos purchaser—typically a white-collar employee who routinely purchases a bag of Doritos as a snack.

Undoubtedly, the primary target market for Doritos is the 18-24 year old demographic. This market is full of people who identify with the "bold" emphasis of the Doritos brand. This demographic group is able to make routine purchases of Doritos chips because the product is cheap and fits within a typical college student's budget. In addition, many Doritos advertisements are made by their consumers—often members of this millennial demographic—which further strengthens brand loyalty to Doritos since now the target market can even further identify with Doritos and their peer-made productions.

As far as psychographics are concerned, this target market perfectly coincides with the "bold" emphasis that Doritos portrays. Many consumers in this market segment want their voices to be heard, and vocalize their opinions through bold, in-your-face acts. Doritos uses consumer-produced advertisements to connect further with their target audience and leave them believing that Doritos understands them and is just like them, especially when taking into account their consumer-produced advertisements.

The secondary target market that Doritos pursues is comprised of mothers and other parents. This target market ranges in age from about 25–40 years old, but has one major common trait: children. Think of a child at the grocery store with his mother pushing the cart down the aisle. Although the child may ask his mother for Doritos, the purchasing decision is ultimately the mother's. Parents buy Doritos for a similar reason as college-aged people: the chips are a delicious and cheap snack. In terms of psychographics, these parents are typically busy with their kids and work schedule and need a cheap and quick way to feed their children, all without sacrificing flavor. Why is this market more relevant than younger children? Children lack the funds to purchase Doritos. Instead, the mother or parent is the most often the purchaser of Doritos for the family. Whether the Doritos are consumed as an after-school snack for the kids, with dip by the husband while watching a sports game, or as a snack in the car on the way to pick up the kids, Doritos is fully aware of the parent-purchaser demographic that undoubtedly boosts sales.

The third market that Doritos targets is their most broad: the routine vending machine purchaser. Think of an average guy who goes to work every day and gets a little hungry about an hour or so before lunch. To hold off his hunger, each day he walks to a vending machine and purchases a bag of Doritos to snack on. Consumers in this demographic are typically educated and have one thing in common besides hunger: routine purchasing. But why does the worker buy Doritos and not some other type of chips or snacks? The worker is primarily attracted to Doritos because of the brand's selection of bold and tasty flavors. When the worker purchases Doritos, he does not hope his taste buds will be satisfied, he knows they will be satisfied. And with a large array of flavors, his taste buds rarely get bored with Doritos. While it is difficult to note the demographics of this target market, it is easy to identify the psychographics. The consumers in this target marker eat Doritos because they are hungry and they know that they enjoy the flavors that Doritos offers. Also, they know that Doritos are readily available in the vending machine for about a dollar. In fact, this whole target market relies on the distribution process of vending machines, as the consumers are primarily purchasing Doritos out of convenience.

Objectives and Strategies Campaign Objectives

By the end of our campaign we want consumers to associate the Doritos brand with the words "bold" and "adventurous." This will allow Doritos to better associated with a strong taste and a bold journey. These associations can lead to an increase in sales, especially among millennials. Our campaign will also increase brand perception, which is always the goal for advertising.

Another one of the goals that we want to accomplish by the end of the campaign is to have a 10% increase in sales at gas stations and convenience stores. This is an attainable goal because this campaign is striving for a very large impact. As will be discussed later, the campaign will include in-store displays at the points of purchase in gas stations and convenience stores on major routes. These displays will easily increase sales and impulsive purchases. We believe our goal of a 10% increase will be reached and is an appropriate target as we are now entering the spring and summer months. In these months, consumers are more likely to be active outside, in the car, and connecting with the brand as a fuel for fun and adventure.

Our campaign also aims to make a larger footprint on social media outlets, including Twitter, Facebook, Instagram, and YouTube. Each social media outlet will be monitored and funnels back to the main Doritos site for redirecting to places to buy Doritos.

For Twitter, we will be following and monitoring our Twitter handle and all Doritos hashtags. We will also work with Doritos to increase the number of user-posted videos, pictures, and status updates retweeted by Doritos to increase the interaction between the company and the consumer. In turn, consumers will feel essential to the brand as individuals.

For Facebook, we will monitor Doritos mentions in status updates and try and set up a Doritos photo shoot. This will allow Doritos fans to have pictures of them posted on the Doritos page and will increase customer involvement.

For Instagram, we will be monitoring photos and on-the-go, easy, and fun recipes that involve Doritos. This will allow customers to trade ideas and good food.

YouTube will be somewhat of a hub and have more focus than the other social media outlets. YouTube is an underutilized social media outlet and can help make the Doritos brand even bigger. Our campaign will use video from people's submissions and posts to demonstrate the strength of the brand and its consumers.

On that same note, if the videos contain enough adequate footage, they could easily be used for more advertising on the bigger scale. Thus in a way making a campaign within a campaign inadvertently that will in the end work wonders. One of these wonders is customers will be highly involved much like the other social medias but putting a video on the TV and advertising is a whole new level.

In the end, our objectives are to make consumers associate the Doritos brand with the words "bold" and "good time." The next objective will be met with the increase in sales by 10% via our last objective. Which is increasing Doritos' social footprint.

Advertising Strategy

The brightly colored bag, the overwhelmingly delicious smell as soon as you open the bag, the cheesy orange triangles, the powder left on your fingertips as you are snacking, the extreme flavor, and the post-snack finger licking session; these are all a part of the Doritos eating experience. From the beginning, Doritos has not settled for ordinary. Doritos is a bold brand that provides the consumer with a unique experience. From the bright, eye-catching bag, to the seasoning left on your fingers, everything that Doritos does is appealing to the consumer and leaves them wanting more. The consumer wants more of the Doritos experience, so let us give it to them.

Doritos appeals to 18–24 year olds who want a voice and are living outside of the norm. Our campaign will target a subset of the Doritos brand's current target audience: millennials aged 18–24 who are most likely working towards a college degree. More specifically, we are going to target those millennials with a desire to travel; those consumers who experience wanderlust and are torn between wanting to travel the world, needing to find a job, and not having the resources to do both.

For this target audience, as discussed above, we will use a variety of social media outlets. However, our main focus for the campaign will be Instagram. Instagram is the best choice for this campaign due to the high involvement of our target market on the app. Of Instagram's 60.3 million users, 27.6% are individuals between the ages of 18 and 24. Instagram allows for communication through hashtags, shared photos, and short videos, all of which are ideal for our campaign.

The main idea behind the campaign is wanderlust—something we all suffer from in our college years. We will target millennials who feel like they do not have the ability to travel the world, but still have a strong desire to do so. Our message is that you do not have to travel to a foreign country to have an adventure; you can find adventure in your own backyard. Doritos wants to help turn any journey into a bold journey.

Using Instagram and the hashtag #DoriTO, we will encourage our bold consumers to take a journey and embrace their adventure. It does not matter where you go; the experience is more important. Take a bold trip, make memories that will last a lifetime, and have Doritos by your side while you are doing it. A bold snack for a bold life.

We will promote a variety of posts that go along with the campaign, including short videos exploring thrilling travel destinations, reposts showcasing consumers who are embarking on bold adventures, and photos of Doritos at different landmarks around the United States. The assortment of posts will be aesthetically pleasing and will appeal to the "roadtripper" in all of us. Listed below are examples of three potential posts for our Instagram account:

A bag of Sweet and Spicy Chili Doritos sitting at the base of the St. Louis Gateway Arch with a photo taken at an angle in order to capture the bag of Doritos and the upward slope of the arch. The caption of the photo will read, "Gateway to the Bold #DoriTOStLouis." A fifteen-second montage of a hand reaching out and holding Nacho Cheese Doritos in a variety of historic attractions around Washington D.C. The caption of the video will read, "Four Score and Seven Chips Ago... #DoriTOWashingtonDC #OriginalRoadtripper." A bag of Cool Ranch Doritos will be sitting in the passenger seat of the car buckled up by the seat belt and the scenery out the window will be beach-like with palm trees. The caption of the photo will read, "This passenger knows how to keep his cool. #DoriTOCalifornia."

We will encourage consumers to document their journeys with the #DoriTO hashtag and then you finding other adventurers traveling to the same destination (e.g., #DoriTOSaltLakeCity, #DoriTOBoston, #DoriTOMiami). By pairing with the smartphone application Waze, we are also able to help consumers reach their destinations. Consumers can enter in their destination and—like a GPS—we will show them the smartest route with the earliest arrival time, will alert them to any accidents or traffic on the way, and will list the most convenient locations to stop for their favorite snack: Doritos. Once the consumer arrives at their destination, we will encourage them to take a "selfie" with their Doritos and show us how amazing their experience is. We will also be pairing with Roadtrippers.com, an online forum that allows consumers to document their trip, find the best travel destinations, and connect with other people seeking a bold journey.

With our engagement on Instagram, posts of original content, and pairing with other web applications, we are taking our previous campaigns to a new level. The goal for this campaign is to encourage interaction with our consumers on social media and, in turn, increase our engagement rate, brand awareness as a bold brand with the Doritos experience, and serve as a reminder to our consumers to purchase our product while they are out and about in turn increasing gas station and convenience store sales. Because we are used to targeting this millennial audience, we are already using our current pool of customers. We are simply transitioning into a more specific psychographic segment of the target audience.

As for our metrics of success, we will begin by looking at our current engagement rate on Instagram: 3.09%. We will also take into consideration our current convenient store and gas station sales and determine how much of an increase in sales we expect throughout the campaign.

The campaign will begin right around the beginning of summer for college students (May 1) and last until the start of the new school year (September 1). At the end of this campaign, we hope to review our data and see a 10% increase in convenience store and gas station sales, a 5% overall increase in sales, and at least a 4% engagement rate on Instagram.

We have a very large vision for this campaign and we want to see it be a large success with our consumers. In order to make this campaign fully successful, I will need a few creative minds, a small budget, and a few tools to help create and inspire the tweets. Listed below are the specifics:

People:
- Social Media Coordinator: A person that will deal directly with Instagram by creating content and engaging with consumers.
- Graphic Designer/Video Production: Someone with a telecommunications background that is able to create visuals, infographics, and videos to send out in our Instagram posts.
- Analyst: We will need someone in charge of pulling data from the stores and staying on top of trends affecting millennials..

Money:
- $8,000 Travel Budget (including gas, hotel, airfare, etc.)
- We will need enough money to cover the cost of salaries for the employees in charge of the campaign.
- The cost of products for giveaways and promotions.

Tools:
Social mention to monitor keywords from over 100 social media sites, Simply measured to see the success of our posts on and outside of Instagram, as well as Nitrogram to get statistics per photo.

This campaign will open the door for a new type of engagement with our consumers. We are allowing for the Doritos experience to be a part of the consumer's personal experiences, and in turn will increase sales and build brand loyalty. I believe this is a minimal cost for all of the benefits that could potentially arise from this campaign. We are raising the bar on our "Bold Experience" and setting standards to which other brands will aspire.

Budget

Wanderlust, a strong desire to travel, also known as something we all experience—especially during the summer months. As a team, Doritos decided that advertising during the months of May, June, July, and August would be the most beneficial for our campaign. Our #DoriTo campaign consists of consumers traveling around the U.S. with their favorite Doritos snack by their side and documenting their road trip with pictures. From there, they will post these photos on their social media with the hashtag #DoriTo followed by the location they had the great fortune of traveling to. Because our campaign is taking place during the summer, which is an ideal time for people outside enjoying the sunshine and not cooped up on the computer and in front of the television, we decided that advertising a few months before and up to summer would be the ideal time to inform our consumers of our upcoming campaign.

It is no secret that Doritos has a large advertising budget. With a parent company as well-known as Frito-Lay, there should be plentiful financial resources for our campaign's budget. After considering the typical cost of Doritos campaigns, we have determined that $10 million would suffice for our marketing budget. As a team, we debated how much money we need to cover each month and each marketing medium. Our breakdown consists of digital, radio, promotions, television, social media, and contingency plan expenditures.

The amounts allotted to each platform are very consistent amounts of money per month. In the four months that our campaign is going to be presented, we chose to spend:

Included below you will find an outline of our budget for the entirety of the campaign and see how it is broken up every month according to each medium.

Television: $4,494,038

Radio: $15,000

Digital: $790,462

Social Media: $2,945,500

Promotions: $755,000

Contingency: $1,000,000

Marketing Expenditures	May	June	July	August	Totals
Television	$2,394,038	$2,100,000	$0	$0	$4,494,038
Radio	$5,000	$5,000	$5,000	$0	$15,000
Digital	$8,700	$390,300	$390,300	$300	$790,462
Social Media	$20,500	$1,451,500	$1,451,500	$21,000	$2,945,500
Promotions	$0	$283,125	$283,125	$188,750	$755,000
Contingency Plan	$250,000	$250,000	$250,000	$250,000	$1,000,000
Total Marketing Spending	$2,678,238	$4,479,925	$2,379,925	$460,050	$10,000,000.00
Company Sales Totals	$108,333,333.00	$108,333,333.00	$108,333,333.00	$108,333,333.00	$433,333,332.00
Marketing as a % Sales	2.47%	4.14%	2.20%	0.42%	2.308%

Figure 13.3. Marketing Expenditures

We have decided to focus on commercials at a national level. Doritos wanted everyone in the United States to see our campaign so that we could deliver effectively and get many people to participate. Based on the viewing habits of our target market, we decided to air our commercials on MTV, Comedy Central, and during *The Voice*. In addition, Doritos chose to advertise on Sirius Radio on a national level to further reach our target market. We also spent our advertising budget on promotions. These promotions include in-store advertisements and giveaways and will keep the community active in our campaign and more likely to participate. Doritos also decided to advertise on social media. The first social media platform we chose was Snapchat. We will make a Snapchat story every week advertising our campaign. Snapchat will be a beneficial component of our campaign because the majority of individuals in our target market use Snapchat. The next social media platform we chose was Instagram. We will post sponsored Instagram photos advertising our ongoing campaign. Other platforms we chose were Twitter, You-Tube, and Buzzfeed. These social media platforms are also widely used by our target market and will help increase involvement in our campaign. Doritos also decided our campaign would benefit from digital advertising, including Google AdWords, banner advertisements, Pandora advertisements, Waze, and the upkeep of our website. All of these platforms provide additional ways to convince our target market to participate in our campaign.

Media Objectives and Strategy

Media Objectives
1. Have people use our hashtag #DoriTo.
2. Increase customer retention.
3. Remind people to buy.
4. Suggest new uses.
5. Build customer demand by 10%.
6. Enhance brand image by increasing net promoter score by 5%.

Primary Target Market
- Millennials.
- 16–24 years old.
- Wanderlust, hankering to travel.
- Looking for excitement, enjoys adventure.
- Taste preference of bold flavors.

Creative Implications

In discussing our media objectives, we decided that our campaign would aim to acquire new customers while keeping existing customers by creating a nationwide campaign that challenges customers to share their Doritos experience through social media mediums. The specific target market for Doritos and this campaign are young adults aging from 16 to 24 years old. As for psychographics, these customers are typically online enthusiasts or gamers that have a bold attitude and excitement within them that coincide with Dorito's bold attitude and flavor. This campaign would build demand for Doritos and ultimately increase revenue while enhancing the brand's image and more and more customers partake in the campaign. Doritos customers desiring to share their Doritos experience on their social media platforms would use creative hashtags linking their location along with a bag of Doritos. For example, if some friends where in Times Square desiring to share their bold experience on Instagram, they could use #DoriTONYC. Perhaps the customer is taking a bold journey to the couch; they could similarly post #DoriTOMyCouch. No matter how far or how bold the journey, Dorito's customers in America could easily find and create hashtags to see how others post their Dorito's experience

To geographically reach across the United States with this campaign and acquire customers, a certain level of frequency is required to raise awareness of the campaign. But is reach or frequency more important for our campaign? In reality, both are very important, but Doritos would benefit more from a campaign focused on frequency. Our goal would be to raise campaign awareness by primarily using a fighting advertising schedule. Frequently advertising is more beneficial to Doritos for boosting brand awareness and will result in the frequent purchase of Doritos chips.

To effectively reach our customers across the nation, our campaign will utilize a mixture of media platforms including television, radio, in store promotional displays, and social media. In using social media, apps like Snapchat will be particularly effective in displaying our campaign on their 'story' feature. This will not only boost awareness of the campaign, but it will remind customers to buy Doritos and increase the brand's image in the minds of consumers. Since we are using a media mix that spans the entirety of the United States, customers will span geographically from the West to East coast.

In designing our creative strategy it became clear that we will need to rely heavily on the use of television for our campaign. This creative implication arises from the fact that advertising on television is both very expensive and very effective. Simply put, advertising on television is a double-edged sword that reaches a large audience and boosts the number of impressions, including our target market, but on the other hand it is the most expensive type of media, and not all of our customers necessarily watch television. By frequently broadcasting our campaign advertisement through networks like Comedy Central and MTV, we will reach our primary target market effectively and will acquire new customers who take an interest in our campaign.

When this campaign takes flight, it is important to inform trade consumers and large distributors of our product about the campaign and urge them to promote it. From Walmart to 7-Eleven, knowledge of the promotion will be advantageous to both Doritos and its trade consumers. In addition, word-of-mouth both inside and outside these organizations will help bolster demand for Doritos, and will increase repeat purchases and impulse purchases. Especially at vending machines, where some consumers make daily purchases and others make impulsive purchases.

Budget Limitations

Because PepsiCo is the parent company of Doritos, our total budget was a logical amount to spend on a four-month campaign. When we formed our budget we decided that allocating our funds evenly across the four months of the campaign would be the most logical way to budget. In actuality, we found that placing our money in different mediums at different times would be more effective in reaching our target market. While maintaining the same percentage of allocated funds in some areas, we modified our flowchart to fit our budget without changing our contingency plan or total budget. The largest portions of our budget went toward television and online/social media advertisements, but these mediums also reach the largest audience. The smallest portion of the budget went toward tangible in-store promotional displays.

Marketing Expenditures	May	June	July	August	Totals
Television	$2,394,038	$2,100,000	$0	$0	$4,494,038
Radio	$5,000	$5,000	$5,000	$0	$15,000
Digital	$8,700	$390,300	$390,300	$300	$790,462
Social Media	$20,500	$1,451,500	$1,451,500	$21,000	$2,945,500
Promotions	$0	$283,125	$283,125	$188,750	$755,000
Contingency Plan	$250,000	$250,000	$250,000	$250,000	$1,000,000
Total Marketing Spending	$2,678,238	$4,479,925	$2,379,925	$460,050	$10,000,000.00
Company Sales Totals	$108,333,333.00	$108,333,333.00	$108,333,333.00	$108,333,333.00	$433,333,332.00
Marketing as a % Sales	2.47%	4.14%	2.20%	0.42%	2.308%

Figure 13.3. Marketing Expenditures (repeated)

Strategy-Media Mix

We will focus the most effort and allocate the most money to television advertising. Television is our primary focus because the most information can be sent through a television ad. Our medium for television will be network and cable TV. More specifically, we will advertise on Comedy Central, MTV, and during the show *The Voice*. All of these advertisements will be distributed nationwide to cover the maximum amount of people.

Our secondary medias encompass radio (through SiriusXM), digital (through Google AdWords, the Waze application, Roadtrippers.com, and Pandora). Social media platforms such as Twitter, YouTube, Instagram, and Buzzfeed Sponsored Articles will also be used.

By focusing on radio with SiriusXM, we will be able to play advertisements over the air on stations that are broadcast across the United States. These advertisements will contribute to our campaign reach and could have an increase in frequency with minimal efforts. Transitioning over to the digital aspect, the same justification exists for Pandora advertisements. Because Pandora is an online radio service, it has the reach of international advertising and can have frequency increased easily. AdWords, Roadtrippers.com, and Waze are very different platforms. With Google AdWords, we will be able to place ads at the top of searched pages that have key words. This will also help the banners on Roadtrippers.com increase the frequency of our advertising message reaching the consumer. With the up-and-coming application Waze, consumers will be able to see advertisements about Doritos. If the advertisements are clicked, they will show the nearest location at which to purchase Doritos.

On the social media standpoint, which is one of the most pertinent to the success of our campaign, we are using Twitter, Instagram, YouTube and Buzzfeed Sponsored Articles. Twitter and Instagram will be able to compare to the success of our television advertisements. Twitter and Instagram are international platforms that tend to be more interactive with consumers on a large scale and make them feel as if they are a part of the Doritos brand. Consumers will also be directly involved with the content that is generated from these social sites; therefore, they will be more willing to involve themselves and participate in the campaign, whether it is through reposts or retweets. YouTube will serve as a great marketing tool as well. With our advertisements running before selected videos, consumers will be entrapped temporarily by our advertisement. Video advertisements present us with opportunities to get more content to our consumers and visually appeal to them. With the Buzzfeed Sponsored Articles, we are penetrating a new market that includes consumers who do not interact on social media, but want to view interesting content.

Scheduling

Television

We want to have a pulsing advertising for Comedy Central, MTV, and *The Voice*. Advertising will start at the beginning of the campaign around the end of April and the beginning of May to increase the frequency of the advertisement. We want to reach at least 25% of our audience with a frequency of around 3-4 advertisements per week. This frequency will stay constant through the end of July, then go to flighting for most of August as the campaign comes to a close with a target of 15% reach and a frequency of 2–3 per week.

Radio and Digital

Our radio and digital marketing efforts will utilize a more continuous advertising strategy. These advertisements will begin in May and continue until the end of the campaign in August to ensure that consumers remain aware of the campaign. We want to reach approximately 15% of our target audience and have a frequency of 5–6 ads per week because radio and digital are less expensive media than TV, but can have more frequency and possibly increase interaction with the brand.

Social Media

For social media, we plan to use a pulsing advertising campaign by keeping weekly updates but increasing advertising on Thursday through Sunday. This strategy will increase the perception of Doritos as a fun and exciting brand that is ready to go when you are, even for a weekend getaway. Our social media advertising will start in May and continue through the first week of August, thus encompassing the majority of the campaign. We want to reach at least 35% of our target audience on these mediums, combined with a frequency of 6–7 ads per week due to the ease of creation and exposure.

Since we have planned a more national campaign and have chosen mediums that are distributed nationally and internationally, there is not much weight that can be shifted. Instead, we are covering all DMA's in a consistent blanket to keep everything equal so that when traveling you feel the consistency of Doritos.

Media Tactics: Specific Vehicle Recommendations

Media Flowchart

 # DoriTO Advertising Campaign
Media Flowchart

Media	May					June				July				Aug					Cost
	2	9	16	23	30	6	13	20	27	3	10	17	24	1	8	15	22	29	**$10,000,000**
Television																			**$4,494,038**
Comedy Central		17 GRPs				17 GRPs													$2,100,000
MTV		15 GRPs				15 GRPs													$2,100,000
The Voice				Finale: 14 million viewers															$294,038
Radio																			**$15,000**
Sirius Radio																			$15,000
Digital																			**$790,462**
Google Adwords	3,000 clicks per month				3,000 clicks per month					3,000 clicks per month				3,000 clicks per month					$1,200
Banner Advertisements (Roadtripper)	3 MM Impressions																		$8,400
Pandora Advertisements							77,000,000 active listeners		77,000,000 active listeners										$530,000
Waze (Map Application)						Audience of 30 million people													$250,000
Website Upkeep																			$862
Social Media																			**$2,945,500**
Snapchat Story																			$1,500,000
Sponsored Instagram Posts							>2,000 comments/likes												$1,000,000
Trending Twitter Topic																			$400,000
Promoted Tweets																			$2,500
Youtube In-Stream						12,886 avg. views per month													$3,000
Buzzfeed Sponsored Article	87.5 MM daily user between 18–34																87.5 MM		$40,000
Promotions						In-store display, contests, give-aways										Winner prize			**$755,000**
Contingency Plan																			**$1,000,000**
Totals																			**$10,000,000**

Figure 13.4. Media Flowchart

Television

Television has always been a reliable source when it came to advertising, whether for a product or for a service. According to an infographic on Forbes.com, television has been so successful in advertising because it has the ability to reach a larger number of people on a national level faster than other sources of advertising. In turn, television advertising is able to build interest and awareness in your brand faster than other methods of advertising.

With all of that in mind, we allocated a large portion of our advertising budget to television advertising. With our target market being college students ages 18-24, we focused primarily on Comedy Central, MTV, and *The Voice*—all shows or networks that hold a large millennial audience.

The price of a 30-second advertisement on Comedy Central averages $28,000. In our media flowchart, we have allocated $2,100,000 to Comedy Central, which in turn will allow us to have 75 advertisements throughout the months of May and June. Because our campaign (#DoriTO) is centered around traveling, we chose the months of May and June because most people will be planning or preparing for their summer trips during these months.

MTV is known world-wide for being a key player in the 18–24 year segment. With its strong position in pop culture and millennial lifestyles, MTV is a main destination for advertisers who are trying to appeal to this segment. Because we are seeking to attract these bold millennials, we have chosen MTV as a source for our advertising as well. We have allocated $2,100,000 for 30-second segments to air throughout the months of May and June. The price of an advertisement on MTV is $15 per 1,000 views. According to NumberOf.Net, 8.5 million people watch MTV one hour per day. Assuming that all 8.5 million viewers that watch MTV per day will see our advertisement, the cost will be $127,500 per advertisement and we will have 16 advertisements.

Our third television advertising platform will be NBC's *The Voice*. The eighth season of *The Voice* will conclude in May 2015. This advertisement will serve as a very effective "beginning" to our campaign. Past finales of *The Voice* brought in an average audience of 14 million viewers. We will have to pay $294,038 for a 30-second advertisement during this program, but we believe that the benefits of such exposure are priceless.

Radio

The cost of an advertisement on SiriusXM radio ranges between $5,000 and $10,000 per week, depending on the popularity on the station and the type of advertisement. For our campaign, we are estimating $5,000 per week for advertising on the "Today's Hits" channel for three weeks. Our radio advertisements will air during the first week of May, the first week of June, and the first week of July. The reach of SiriusXM radio is 51 million listeners. Even if our campaign garnered only 10% of that reach, we would still be able to reach an audience of 5.1 million listeners.

Digital

The internet provides advertisers with a variety of cost-effective solutions to their advertising needs. For our campaign, we want to gain a large online presence and therefore consider it very beneficial to allocate a large portion of our budget to digital advertising, as well as social media. According to the Pew Research Center, 93% of young adults are going online.

As of 2013, 10% of the United States population was made up of young adults ages 18–24. Ten percent does not sound like a large portion of the United States, but when you think of it in terms of 31.5 million people, you realize the impact that the age group has or could have on your advertising efforts and see how it directly correlates with being online.

Google AdWords

We have all experienced this form of advertising at some point in our lives. You go to a search engine and type in a phrase or keyword and you receive millions of results. However, at the top of the page, there are a select few results that stand out from the rest and seem to be more appealing and relate more closely to what you searched. These results are directly related to Google AdWords. By choosing terms such as "DoriTO Campaign," "Dorito Roadtrip," "Roadtrip," and "Summer Trip," we are able to appear as a preferred result for those who are either looking for our campaign or are looking to travel over the summer months. With Google AdWords, you are able to set a daily budget. By setting our budget at $10 per day, we are able to stay relevant on Google for 120 days, which is the duration of our campaign, and only spend $1,200 out of our budget. We are going to be focusing on the cost per click strategy so that we can drive traffic to our website. See below for an example from Google explaining the pricing layout for Google AdWords:

Example:
Let's say your cost per click is $0.10 on average, and you'd like around 100 clicks per day. You might budget $10 per day.

Using this example, here's how you'd figure out your daily budget:

$0.10 × 100 = $10 per day (Cost per click × Clicks per day = Daily budget)

Banner Advertisements on Roadtrippers.com

As seen on Roadtrippers.com, co-founders James Fisher and Tatiana Parent suffer from an incurable case of wanderlust. So, they decided to design a web and mobile platform that streamlines discovery, planning, booking, and navigation into one engaging road trip planner. What better way to promote our adventurous, traveling Doritos campaign than team up with a road trip planning online application?

The average CPM for online banner advertisement is around $2.80. According to Roadtrippers.com' Press Kit, they receive three million unique site visits monthly. Taking this number and comparing it to the CPM shows us that advertising monthly on Roadtrippers.com will cost $8,400. To best utilize these resources, we decided to advertise heavily throughout the month of May—while people are planning their summer road trips—to hopefully reach three million of these individuals.

Waze Map Application

The majority of millennials were not brought up being taught how to use an Atlas to navigate their trips. Most young adults utilize the extraordinary navigational powers of a GPS. Google created an application called Waze that allows users to not only navigate, but also alerts users to sites of interest, traffic, construction, and the presence of police officers ahead. Like Google AdWords, Waze allows advertisers to set a monthly budget and then the advertisement will appear as frequently as possible within your given budget. Waze is measured by each 1,000 impressions, and with an audience of 30 million people, we are able to estimate that we are going to need to allocate $250,000 for advertisements on this application.

Pandora Advertisements

There are many different options for advertising on Pandora. The best use of the company for our campaign is the "Audio Everywhere" option. This type of advertisement includes a banner, tile photo, and an audio message. The audio message will contain a call to action (e.g., "click on the screen or visit our website for more information"). Having an "Audio Everywhere" option showcasing our campaign with a call to action to our campaign website or our social media pages is the most effective way to inform the listener.

The reach of Pandora was 77 million active listeners at the end of May 2014, which was an increase of 9% from 70.8 million during May 2013. If Pandora continues to follow this growth trend, it is possible that Pandora will reach 83.9 million people this May. Following the CPM average of $6.85, we have allocated $530,000 to advertise heavily on Pandora for the months of June and July when people will be traveling and wanting to listen to music in the car.

Social Media

Twitter

Social media is the second largest marketing expenditure in our campaign. We have allocated almost three million dollars to make sure that we are successful on all platforms of social media. One of the most important platforms is Twitter. When looking at options for advertising on Twitter, we found benefits in them all. Twitter offers three types of advertising options: promoted tweets, promoted accounts, and promoted trends. The first two cost between $.50–$4.00 per engagement, and promoted trends cost $200,000 per day. Promoted tweets are tweets you have already tweeted that you wish to promote.

As a team, we decided that the best ways to help promote our campaign were to invest in promoted tweets and trending topics. We are going to pay to have #DoriTO a trending topic on Twitter at the beginning of June and at the beginning of July. The cost of promoting the hashtag is $200,000, so our investment will be $400,000. We are going to use promoted tweets at the end of each month and two promoted tweets at the end of August to showcase the success of our campaign.

Following the formula of SimplyMeasured, to find the engagement rate for a brand you need to add up the total likes and comments on the last ten posts and divide by ten to get the average engagement per post. For Doritos, the average engagement per post totals 563.1. Assuming that the cost is $0.50 per engagement, that is approximately $281.50 per promoted tweet. Because social media is such a large portion of this campaign, we have allocated $500 per promoted tweet and our total budget for promoted tweets is $2,500.

YouTube In-Stream Advertisement

Two of the most watched categories on YouTube are Entertainment (9,816 view average) and Travel (3,070 view average). There are many different options for advertising on YouTube, but we felt that the best way to utilize our money would be to use in-stream advertisements. If we advertise heavily in entertainment and travel videos during June and July—when people are most likely to YouTube music videos or travel destinations in the car while they are driving—we could potentially have an average reach of 12,886 per month. The cost to advertise on YouTube with this method is $0.20 per view.

Buzzfeed Sponsored Article

If there is one that I personally remember from my time at Ball State University, it is the amount of time that I spent on Buzzfeed during and outside of class; it was not just me—all of my friends would partake in Buzzfeed as well. We thought a Buzzfeed Sponsored Article would be a great way to explain and preview the campaign in May and a great way to showcase our success at the end of August when everyone is coming back to school from their adventures.

Buzzfeed has 175,000,000 unique monthly users and 50% of those users are between the ages of 18-34. If we could even reach 20% of that 87,500,000 we could have an audience of 17,500,000 for our Buzzfeed articles. The cost of an article with this much reach is $20,000 per article.

Instagram

Recent feedback from brands that participated in the trial stated that the CPM costs to advertise with Instagram are much higher than the cost to advertise on other social sharing sites and networks. The lower end of monthly pricing is estimated around $350,000, but pricing can reach $1 million. For the sake of our campaign, I estimated that our average per month would be $500,000.

The ability to promote our campaign and showcase our consumers' pictures on Instagram will be hugely important for our campaign. Because Instagram only allows you to view one photo at a time as you are scrolling through your feed, social media users are engaging or focusing on each post and understanding our message. Brands that have used Instagram as a way to promote their business found that they typically yield thousands of photo likes and drastically increase engagement and awareness.

Snapchat

Last on our lineup of social media is Snapchat. We are hoping to be featured on the newest addition of Snapchat: Discover. One day on the Discover page costs approximately $750,000. We have allocated $1,500,000 to Snapchat advertising so that we can be featured on the Discover page once in mid-June and in once mid-July. Advertising on Snapchat will allow users around the world to interact with our brand and see our campaign in action.

References

1. Detroit: Gale, 2007. 583-586. *Gale Virtual Reference Library*. Web. 15 Feb. 2015.

2. "About Manual CPC bidding," *Google Adwords*, accessed May 11, 2016, https://support.google.com/adwords/answer/2464960?hl=en.

Image Credits

Fig. 13.2a : Copyright © Depositphotos/urbanbuzz.

Fig 13.2b: Copyright © Depositphotos/homank76.

Fig. 13.2c: Copyright © Depositphotos/akulamatiau.

Fig. 13.2d: Copyright © Depositphotos/rookman48.

Fig. 13.3: Statista, "Marketing Expenditures," http://www.statista.com/statistics/189614/top-cracker-brands-in-the-united- states/

Fig. 13.3: Lexis Nexis, "Marketing Expenditures," http://w3.nexis.com/sources/scripts/info.pl?7088

Fig. 13.4: "Media Flow Chart," http://www.activemedia-guide.com/mrksh_profile.htm.

WORKS CITED

America's greatest brands. N.p., n.d. Web. 14 Feb. 2015. http://www.americasgreatestbrands. com/volume6/pdf/Doritos.pdf.

Bhasin, K. (2012, December 19). The Psychological Secrets Behind Nacho Cheese Doritos. Retrieved February 15, 2015, from http://www.businessinsider.com/ nacho-cheese-doritos-brand-2012-12

Bruce, H., & USA, T. (n.d). Taco Bell + Doritos = success?. *USA Today.*

Chau, B. (2014). Chippin Away Like Frito-Lay. *SuccessPenPal.* Retrieved from http://success-penpal.com/chippin-away-like-frito-lay-environmental-factors/

DOL. N.p., n.d. Web. 14 Feb. 2015. http://www.dol.gov/whd/minwage/america.htm.

Doritos. (n.d.). Retrieved from http://www.conservapedia.com/Doritos

Doritos Launches First Global Campaign. (n.d.). Retrieved February 15, 2015, from http:// adage.com/article/news/doritos-launches-global-campaign/240173/

Frito-Lay Company History. (n.d.). Retrieved from http://www.fundinguniverse.com/ company-histories/frito-lay-company-history/

Frito-Lay Names CMO. (n.d.). Retrieved February 15, 2015, from http://www.adweek.com/ news/advertising-branding/frito-lay-names-cmo- 100547

Frito-Lay Purpose. (n.d.). Retrieved from http://www.fritolay.com/purpose

Kellogg to Buy Procter & Gamble's Pringles Group. (2012, February 15). Retrieved from http:// dealbook.nytimes.com/2012/02/15/kellogg-to-buy-procter-gambles- pringles-group/

Leading cracker brands sales of the U.S., 2012 | Statistic. (n.d.). Retrieved from http://www. statista.com/statistics/189614/top-cracker-brands-in-the-united- states/

Lexica list. N.p., n.d. Web. 14 Feb. 2015. http://lexicalist.com/search.cgi?s=doritos&d=age

Reyes, S. (2006). After Sales Dip, Frito-Lay Fires Up Doritos Brand. *Brandweek, 47*(2), 6.

Risland, Susan. "Frito-Lay Inc." *Encyclopedia of Major Marketing Campaigns.* Vol. 2. Detroit: Gale, 2007. 583-586. *Gale Virtual Reference Library.* Web. 15 Feb. 2015.

Strachan, M. (n.d.). Doritos Locos Tacos Sales Pass $1 Billion (Unrelated: We're All Doomed). Retrieved February 15, 2015, from http://www.huffingtonpost.com/2013/10/16/doritos-locos-tacos-sales- billion_n_4110741.html

Thompson, S. (2002). Doritos to Net teens. *Advertising Age, 73*(3), 8.

"Top Cracker Brands, 2013." Market Share Reporter. Ed. Robert S. Lazich and Virgil L. Burton, III. 25th ed. Farmington Hills, Mich.: Gale Group, 2015. 838 pp. 2 vols. Gale Directory Library. Gale. Ball State University. 13 Feb. 2015 http://find.galegroup.com/gdl/ start.do?prodId=GDL.

"Top Potato Chip Brands, 2013." Market Share Reporter. Ed. Robert S. Lazich and Virgil L. Burton, III. 25th ed. Farmington Hills, Mich.: Gale Group, 2015. 838 pp. 2 vols. Gale Directory Library. Gale. Ball State University. 15 Feb. 2015 http://find.galegroup.com.proxy. bsu.edu/gdl/start.do?prodId=GDL.

Yager, S. (2014). DORITOS LOCOS TACOS. *Atlantic, 313*(6), 94

5 Lessons In Participatory Marketing From Doritos' "Crash The Super Bowl" And CMO Ann Mukherjee. (2012, February 03). Retrieved February 15, 2015, from http://www. fastcocreate.com/1679605/5-lessons-in-participatory-marketing-from-doritos-crash-the-super-bowl-and-cmo-ann-mukherjee

CPSIA information can be obtained
at www.ICGtesting.com
Printed in the USA
LVHW06s2000050718
582819LV00001B/6/P